INSURGENT METAPHORS
ESSAYS IN CULTURE AND CLASS

INSURGENT METAPHORS

ESSAYS IN CULTURE AND CLASS

Pothik Ghosh

INSURGENT METAPHORS: ESSAYS IN CULTURE AND CLASS
Pothik Ghosh

First Published, 2010

ISBN (Pb)

Published by
AAKAR BOOKS
28 E Pocket IV, Mayur Vihar Phase I, Delhi-110 091
Phone : 011-2279 5505 Telefax : 011-2279 5641
aakarbooks@gmail.com; www.aakarbooks.com

Printed at
Mudrak, Delhi-110 091

To Paramita, who kept her self-expression in check so that I could give mine

Contents

Acknowledgements 9
Epigraph 11
Introduction 13
1. In Search of Class 31
2. Fascism and a Marxist Praxis of Art 43
3. Academics, Politics and Class Struggle 76
4. The Siren Songs of Neo-traditionalism 90
5. Akhtaruzzaman Elias: Beyond the Lived Time of Nationhood 106
6. Kafka and the Question of Revolutionary Subjectivity 150
7. Media and the Indian State: On the Draft Broadcasting Services Regulation Bill, 2006 162
8. The Blind Art of the Concrete 174
9. In Defence of Hamas 178
10. Sri Lanka: Genocide and Other Majoritarian Falsehoods 186
11. Fascism in its Liberal Womb 194
12. Lalgarh beyond Maoism, Maoism beyond Lalgarh 199
13. Three Fragmentary Theses on the Politico-theoretical Problematic posed by the Current Phase of the Indian Maoist Movement for Working Class Politics 207

Acknowledgements

Acknowledging friends, family and fellow-travellers has become an indispensable ritual in modern publishing. It is a device by which the writer—otherwise immersed in the self-centred, almost arrogant, ethics of individuated production of autographed literature—shows himself to be capable of humility, thus bolstering, paradoxically enough, precisely the authorial self he condescends to efface. It is a gesture of humanisation where there can actually be none. But a work, any work, cannot plausibly be imagined as an extraordinary feat by an individual. More so a book such as this one that claims to be an expression of a political ethics of non-competitive, unalienated collectivity. An individual writer is merely the contingent agency of discourse whose locus is always the collective. As far as this book is concerned that has really been the case. My fidelity to the actual condition of possibility of this book allows me to fulfil the ritual of acknowledgements only by reanimating that ritual to transform it into an authentic act of good faith. This book is truly the product of a collective enterprise. That I have been its writer is a contingent detail that gives me a sense of happiness and pride. And it is this pride and happiness that I wish to share with my "party of the concept".

Comrade Ganeshan of CPI(ML)-Liberation would be the first among them. It is to him I owe the realisation that practice of theory for a partisan has to be much more than merely a matter of private amateurish pursuit.

Anuradha and Ardhendu, thanks to whom I learnt that the complications of theory in politics are not merely theoretical.

Ravi, for being an unobtrusive sounding board for many of the ideas here.

Mr K.K. Saxena of Aakar Books for daring to imagine that this book can be a viable business proposition.

Dr Nagpal, for helping me to make theory the innerness of my experience.

My sister Mampia, whose active interest in my work, not despite but because of her training in the mathematical sciences, inspires in me the belief that an encyclopaedic possibility can yet be retrieved from this late capitalist epoch of abject fragmentation and alienation.

Alok and Saroj, for giving me hope that this book has a future and a collectivity.

Paresh and Satyabrata, for their constant transference of youthful romance and impetuousness of thought on to my being.

Najeeb, for effecting a rather productive encounter between Adornoesque Critical Theory and my Leninism. An encounter that has marked us both.

Manash, for his constant Foucauldian hectoring that forced my Marxism to turn more self-reflexive.

TK, for being the last true liberal amid the debris of a decadent and decaying liberalism.

Amrith, for inspiring me with his belief in the ascetic courage of ideas.

Last but not least, fellow-heretic Pratyush. Our relationship has been one of both combat and dialogue, and something that is much more than a sum of these two parts. This book is, beside other things, primarily an embodiment of that brotherhood of grace.

Epigraph

"The weapon of criticism cannot, of course, replace criticism of the weapon, material force must be overthrown by material force; but theory also becomes a material force as soon as it has gripped the masses. Theory is capable of gripping the masses as soon as it demonstrates *ad hominem*, and it demonstrates *ad hominem* as soon as it becomes radical."

—Karl Marx, *A Contribution to the Critique of Hegel's Philosophy of Right*

Introduction

The international financial crisis has proved, if such proof were necessary, that the politics of proletarian revolution is anything but an outmoded project. The empirical actuality of the crisis is symptomatic of the possible actuality of revolution. This revolution, which has always been alive in the womb of capital, is now rearing to break free. The financial crisis is the first bout of labour pain that indicates the time of its birth is nigh. And yet the situation remains despairing. The Marxist theory of the science of revolution—which is supposed to grasp this possibility and in the process catalyse its transformation into an actuality—appears to be in no shape to guarantee its rendezvous with itself.

Marxism's cultural turn, which has been the dominant theoretical modality of its operation over at least the past four decades, continues to belie the hope it had initially held out on that score. The promise that such a move would eventually steer Marxism out of its purported ontological crisis—which is essentially the outcome of the reduction of a critical science to a doctrinaire communistology—is on the verge of a miscarriage. That is certainly the case, at least, in sub-continental South Asia. Unsurprisingly, therefore, 'culturally-turned' Marxism survives as the sign of the very crisis it was meant to surpass. Its canonisation within the academia, and beyond, as a mere analytic of culture has led to the blurring of politico-ideological lines. The quietist impulse that this theory of the science of revolution has, as a consequence, come to share with so-called poststructuralism implies its complete detachment from all notions and conceptions of class and class action.

The 13 essays that comprise this book are envisaged as a small attempt from South Asia—where communitarian postcolonialism and 'Marxist' culturalism constitute the most respectable trend in radical theory—to somewhat remedy the situation. Culled from at least three left-wing journals (*Correspondence*, *New Correspondence* and *Radical Notes*), where they were first published between 2003 and 2010, the essays collectively articulate a thematic of restoring the conception of class to the idea of culture. I must, however, state at the very outset that this *restorative* endeavour is not some exercise in *revanchist* 'Marxism'. The concept of class in which the theoretical analysis and practice of culture is sought to be grounded here has nothing in common with the reified sociologies of class that constitute the existential upholstery of various communist (read communistological) sects, all of which call themselves communist parties by claiming for their respective sectarian sociology the truth of class.

The formulation of class at work here is, if anything, constitutive of an attempt to critically decimate such sectarian hypostatisation of a highly scientific concept and, in the process, supersede the false identitarian dichotomy between class and culture. A dichotomy on which both the *cultural turners* and the *communistologists* have thrived as sterile sects. The overcoming of this binary has involved the redefinition of the two ideas through an essential reconfiguration of the existing relationship between them. Thus, class and culture, contrary to the prevailing doxa of radical theory and politics, are not competing categorial forms. Instead, class must be seen as the constitutive logic of culture, even as culture is envisaged as an expression of the logic of class. It is this theoretically reconstituted relation between class and identity (or culture) that is posed by 'In Search of Class'—the essay with which this book opens and which was first published in September 2004 in what was the first and last issue of *New Correspondence*.

In the light of this recast relationship, the attempt to situate culture in class would by no means amount to subsumption of one *a priori* ontology by another. Instead, it would imply the conceptual discernment of a form (culture) in terms of its inseparable, sedimental logic (class). The question before such a theoretical operation is not how to subordinate, for instance, the question of tribal identity to that of the worker, which is one of the key reified sociologisations of class, but to see what is the logic that is posited in the assertion of both the tribal and worker identities (cultural forms) in their respective conjunctural contexts.

Culture is clearly nothing less than the totality of human life itself. Culture is how society—human beings in their social existence—manifests itself. To that extent, culture is the attitude and conception that denizens of a social order have towards that order, their existence within and as part of it and thus towards the social relations that constitute the social formation in question.

In other words, culture is the manifest form of transactions and intercourse among people in a social formation. It is an expression and embodiment of social relations themselves. Such social relations, in a modern capitalist order, are constitutive of a hierarchical and, therefore, inegalitarian society. And the culture, or the ensemble of attitudes towards prevailing social relations, that emanates from such a society, even among those who are disgruntled by their positions within it, are hegemonic.

Karl Marx wrote in his preface to *A Contribution to the Critique of Political Economy*: "In the social production of their existence, men inevitably enter into definite relations, which are independent of their will, namely relations of production appropriate to a given stage in the development of their material forces of production." And this determination and subjugation of the independent human will by an attitude that stems from the necessity of producing and perpetuating human (read social) existence is what underpins the hegemonic character of culture of modern capitalist societies.

Such hegemonic relations, needless to say, strengthen the political economy of modern capitalism by concentrating political and economic power in favour of classes whose existence as such is contingent on the survival and success of the socio-economic order in question. Resistance and struggle against such concentration of socio-political power often becomes, as a consequence, intrinsic to the survival of all other members of society. In that context, resistance generates a new, critical attitude towards prevailing social relations and thereby posits, even embodies, in terms of real lived experience an alternative horizon of social existence and, well, culture itself.

The class location, or orientation, of a culture (form) can be ascertained by examining whether that particular cultural form, in its existence in the objectivity of its conjunctural context, asserts its truth as the discursivity of its formal being; or affirms the truth in terms of its formation as an expression of critique and autonomy with regard to the externalised determination (representation) of another cultural form, and the dualising and discursive horizon that such representative determination is constitutive of. The class logic of the first, which engenders duality and value creation, would be bourgeois while that of the second, given that it posits itself in terms of its critical autonomous impulse of formation, would be the proletarian logic of destruction of value creation and thus duality. This latter logic of proletarian culture is nothing but the logic of critique of political economy.

Of course, forms will be forms and will as such, therefore, always be *identifiable* in the discursivity of their formal beings. Therefore, revolutionary working-class culture would be one that not only objectively functions as an embodiment of critique but also self-reflexively eschews the discursivity of its form to subjectively grasp and express itself in terms of its objective logic of critique and autonomy, whose determinate enunciation has impelled its formation in that determinate specificity.

The class character of a culture is, therefore, clearly not to be gauged in terms of how effectively a certain culture can be pressed, in a rather instrumentalised fashion, into the service of another socio-cultural form that goes by the name of class. The trick, instead, is to figure out that character on the basis of how a cultural form is positioned in the objectivity of its situation. That is, whether its situation is as a critical manifestation of the mobile, processual essence of the real, thereby implying continuous deconstitution and reconstitution of forms because of a centrifugal, decentring operation; or whether it is envisaged in its objectivity as a legitimising centre—perhaps even a 'democratic' one in the case of multiculturalism—to express centripetality by repressing the centrifugal logic of its formation. If it is the former, then the culture in question is clearly an expression of the proletarian logic of critical autonomy, whereas the latter would make it into an embodiment of the status-quo conserving, hegemonic culture of the bourgeoisie. It is this constant and recursive dialectic between centrifugality and centripetality that transforms what is proletarian culture of resistance at one moment into a culture of conservation in the next. In such circumstances, the project this book articulates cannot be one that essentialises class, but has to be one that seeks to constantly locate the tendential and mobile essence of class in cultures as they move through various spatio-temporalities to constitute themselves.

In this sense, a culture that does not expresses itself as a form in an absolute sense, but poses its formation to affirm singular autonomy as a critique of a system of cultural forms and its constitutive logic of duality and representation becomes an expression of the logic of the working-class as a class-for-itself, or the logic of socialist production. Therefore, such a cultural form, insofar as it embodies and encapsulates the logic of critical negation of autonomy-denying cultural forms and their logical horizon of duality and discursivity, even as it asserts in that same movement its autonomous, counter-discursive singularity, is insurgent. What distinguishes the theorisation of such insurgent cultures from so-called critical theory is the fact that such theoretical insurgency is, unlike critical theory, not merely a negationist analytic manoeuvre vis-à-vis a discursive formation, but is also an articulation of the affirmativeness of autonomy inherent in such critical negation. Thus, such insurgent forms become crucial not merely because their existence as forms negate other discursivity-constituting forms, but because they posit the logic of critical (negative) autonomy (affirmative) in its entirety. That renders those theoretically conceived insurgent forms—as far as their formality in the determinateness of the theoretical moment is concerned—fragile. So, those insurgent cultures or forms are, for the purposes of the project this book seeks to found, less forms in the sense of doctrinal concepts. They are, in fact, more like forms that allude metaphorically to a self-constituting essence of critical autonomy even as they posit their own negation as formalised discursive systems. This process of self-negation, in its dialectical turn, constitutes and poses, yet again, that logic of non-representative, critically expressive autonomous singularity. That has led me to conceive of such theoretical constructions and expressions of critical, working-class cultures as insurgent metaphors.

Therefore, hegemonic, bourgeois culture is the materialised expression of hierarchical social relations, wherein such relations and their hierarchical configuration are fixed through the stabilisation of the discursivity of the form in and as which the architectonic of those relations emerged. In such circumstances, the materialised forms that emerge as the determinate embodiment of the logic of critique of such hierarchised social relations, their variously formalised configurations and the general logic of discursivity those configurations exhibit are proletarian cultures. Such proletarian cultural forms pose—through their formational logic of critical autonomy—a logical horizon of free association. This horizon of free association, given that it is formed in and positioned as a critique of a centred and established system and its constitutive logic of discursivity, cannot be conceived of as a traditional system governed by the ethics of juridical fixity and, therefore, has no systemic stability. Its existence (actually emergence) as a zone of, what Louis Althusser termed, "encounter" can only be realised in and through a critical unravelling of a horizon of discursivised, and thus stabilised and hierarchised, necessity. To that extent, it is a perpetually self-constituting zone of excess with regard to stabilising systems and the discursivity constitutive of such stabilisation.

A Marxian revolutionary praxis of culture then is one that envisages culture not as a formal system but as a weapon of criticism constitutive of that act. Clearly, a Marxist praxis has to envisage culture not as given forms, which lend themselves to instrumentalised marshalling, but forms grasped and articulated in terms of the logic of their formation or production. That praxis must, in its moment of theoretical analysis, logically extend to pre- and non-Marxian cultures as well to make sense of them not in terms of what their constituent forms say but how, why and under what objective circumstances they say what they say. Such a type of theorisation yields unto us the truth of concepts of cultures, not in terms of the discursivity of their forms, but in terms of the critical logic (or not) of their determinate formation. The worth of such *logical* truth—outside the determinate moment of the concepts and forms formed by that logic—lies in the fact that it is meant to be recognised as something to be refounded in the determinate quest for autonomy through critique in other junctures of concrete contradictions. Thus in a Marxist praxis of culture, a form has no eternal validity as that form beyond the determinate moment of its emergence as an expression of the logic of critical autonomy. Its only validity, beyond the determinate moment of its emergence, is what it has to say about the generalised critical logic of its formation in the historical specificity of its moment of contradiction, duality and externalised determination. As a result, there can be no repertoire of a priori or transhistorical concepts and forms that is freely available for a Marxist praxis of culture for all seasons.

The theoretical forms that encapsulate the critique of the academically discursivised formation called culture—which connotes merely forms and products of the arts and the crafts such as music, art, literature and their various genres and forms—are, in their determinate emergence, doubtless expressions of the logic of critical autonomy. But such theoretical forms, left to themselves, would be no more than mere analytics of an academicised, canonised culture. Unless, of course, the implication that such analysis of academicised culture has for moments outside the determinateness of the academy and its discursive formation are grasped. The importance of the theoretical forms in and through which the critique of the academically discursivised formation of culture is expressed has to be understood not merely in terms of what those theoretical forms say by way of their critical-theoretical analysis of various dimensions of canonically discursivised culture, but how constitutive of the determinate emergence of such critical-theoretical analysis is the quasi-historical, universal logic of critical autonomy. Something that, in terms of its pure logicality, has a bearing for all concrete junctures of duality and discursivity in their respective determinateness. Thus a critical-theoretical analysis of academically discursivised formation of culture that is able to self-reflexively grasp its determinate formation in terms of expressing the quasi-historical, universal logic of critical autonomy and articulate it, rises above its academic-analytic confines to become a conceptual bearer of the logical universality of critical autonomy for all other junctures of duality and domination. It is in those terms that the second essay in the book—'Fascism and a Marxist Praxis of Art' (*Correspondence*, September 2003) – seeks to comprehend the various forms and genres of artistic and literary practices.

Clearly, the theoretical operation of conceptualising cultures or forms in terms of discerning the generalised logic of critical autonomy as the formational essence of those cultures and forms in the determinateness of their specific moments of enunciation transforms theory into a new paradigm of political ethics, which is meant to yield a programme for generalisation of that logic of critical autonomy across various moments of duality and contradiction through its determinate re-enactment in the specificity of those locations. That ensures concepts produced through theorisation are not, as is the traditional wont of theory, condemned to reproduce truth-forms particular to certain moments as the discursivity of a truth that is transhistorically 'universal', but rather become the procedure that facilitates the constant quest for enacting the truth of the logic of critical autonomy in the determinateness of multiple junctures of duality and contradiction. Revolutionary theory, in the specific Leninist sense, is precisely that. And there are two, dialectically integrated, modalities of this theoretical practice: that of the act of expressing critical autonomy in the determinate moment of theory; and then envisaging the form of that counter-discursive, autonomous act as the trace of that act as it occurred in the determinateness of the theoretical moment, and conceptualise that trace as the bearer of the quasi-historical, universal logic of critical autonomy for the determinate moment of pragmatics. So, while the first modality of revolutionary theory is an act in the moment of theory, the second is the theorisation of this act of theory, in terms of its determinate enunciation as the universal logic of critical autonomy, for its reclamation through an act determinate to the moment of pragmatics. This second modality of revolutionary theory—which is intrinsic to the reconstitution of the traditional paradigm of theory as discursivity into a new paradigm of theory as a politico-ethical position of critique—is both a preparation for and an anticipation of the revolutionary rupture in the concrete conditions of living of the working masses.

It has been my attempt in all the essays contained in this book to situate and articulate the cultural turn in Marxism within this register of theory as a political ethics of generalised critique and rupture. For, that is arguably the dimension that academicised radical theory and canonised 'Marxist' culturalism has sought to cleanse culturally-turned Marxism of in the process of institutionalising it. My contention is that the radical protocols of theoretical practice—from critical theory to anti-philosophical expressionism—within the discursive domain of cultural theory, emerged as and through acts of counter-discursive critical autonomy in the determinate terrain formed in the process of envisaging culture as a discursively delimited object of analysis. But that is not all. I would further argue that those ostensibly radical theoretical protocols, when they are seen in terms of their emergent logic of counter-discursivity in the determinateness of the moment of cultural theory, clearly imply the displacement of the terrain of the counter-discursive, critically autonomous act from the moment of discursivised theory to that of pragmatics. That, at least, would be the case if the radical-theoretical protocols are resituated within the modality of theory as a political ethics of generalisation of the logic of critique and rupture. For, then the protocols would not merely be seen as such but also as conceptual encapsulations of the universalising logic of the act of critical, counter-discursive autonomy, which impelled the emergence or formation of those protocols in the determinateness of the moment of theory.

It is precisely on account of the failure to carry this implication through that modes of enacting the logic of critical, counter-discursive autonomy in the moment of discursivised theory have become congealed analytics or conceptually frozen pedagogical epistemologies. This has led to the conflation of the universal essence of critical, counter-discursive autonomy with its form of appearance, and its discursivity, in the theoretical moment. That, needless to say, has meant that those protocols of so-called radical theory have belied their own logic of critical autonomous and counter-discursive emergence on the determinate terrain of canonised cultural theory.

In view of such an understanding of the cultural turn, my engagement with the academic, and academicised, cultural turners could hardly have been one of downright hostility and rejection. It has clearly been determined by a strange mix of dialogue and combat. The dialogic convergence—which is evident in the essays here borrowing concepts, concerns and themes heavily from their canon—is the sharpest when it comes to acknowledging the validity of the idea of theoretical practice. That stems from envisaging the theoretical level of determination as a relatively autonomous level for the enactment of the logic of critical autonomy. Yet, I hope they find my criticism of their 'melancholic' and counterrevolutionary quietism, vis-à-vis the moment of political pragmatics uncomfortably searing. In 'Academics, Politics, Class Struggle'—which is based on the notes of a lecture I gave at Hindu College (Delhi University) on March 4, 2010, and which was published in *Radical Notes* on May 2, 2010—the digits of this critical engagement with the 'melancholic' and quietist subjectivity of the academicised radical theory are explicated.

In 'The Siren Songs of Neo-traditionalism' (*Correspondence*, May 2003), I extend my criticism of academicised radical theory to communitarian postcolonialism and the project of subalternity by taking polemical issue with the attempt of an academic tendency of radical theory to reconceptualise the socio-political via its supposed critique of Marxism. The underlying premise of this essay is that the concept of subalternity, which is in vogue as much outside the academia as within it, theorises opposition to epistemic and administrative centering of knowledge and politics respectively in terms of discursivity of socio-political forms that embody and articulate such opposition. It does not envisage those forms, which real culturally-turned Marxism would, as concepts that encapsulate the universalising logic of critical, counter-discursive autonomy that resulted in their formation in the determinateness of the respective specificity of their socio-political and/or epistemological locations. Such a Marxist conceptualisation would transform the locus of opposition—which communitarian postcolonialism and theorists of subalternity have theoretically fixed as the discursivised position of antithetical opposition—into a sociologically provisional locus of expressing the logic of critical, counter-discursive autonomy that supersedes the centre (political and/or epistemic) and its constitutive contradiction or antinomy (the subaltern) by collapsing them into a synthetic singularity that would preclude all duality and thus centering.

That our postcolonialists have sought to turn their absolutely valid criticism of the reified communistological ontology of Marxism into a rejection of Marxism *per se* is on account of their unwillingness, or inability, to see Marxism as a science of constantly self-constituting rupture and critical singularity and synthesis. It is this that enables us to break with the subalternity-producing horizon of epistemology and administrative anti-politics—under which must be subsumed the communistological ontology of Marxism—thereby abolishing both the representative and discursive centre, and its constitutive subalternity. The scientificity of Marxism, as the essay in question seeks to indicate, is contingent not on this or that ontology and their respective epistemic discursivity. Marxism is a science precisely because it is not an ontological fixity but is both a quasi-historical and quasi-objective tendential logic of immanent critique, and the conceptualised procedure of locating that logic in the determinate diversity and mobility of contradictory junctures. It is the failure to grasp the scientificity of Marxism in those terms that has led to this perilously fraught conception of subalternity, brushing the term against the grain of its first theoretical deployment by Antonio Gramsci in his *Prison Notebooks* as purely an Aesopian, censor-eluding substitute for conceptualising that critical autonomous logical tendency called the proletariat. Thus subalternity, in terms of its modality of operation within the discourse of communitarian postcolonialism, has come to be a formally discursivised concept that has fixed sociological and/or ethnic correlates. Clearly, subalternity, in spite of its radical oppositional tenor, is a concept of culture/identity that articulates the bourgeois class logic of discursivity and centering.

What I propose in 'Academics, Politics and Class Struggle' by way of re-envisaging the modalities of radical theoretical practice as conceptual encapsulations of the universalising logic of critical, counter-discursive autonomy—something that would lead to the unfolding of the subjectivity of radical theoretical practice into a subjectivity seeking revolutionary rupture in the moment of pragmatics—is terminologically rendered as "academics beyond academia". 'Akhtaruzzaman Elias: Beyond the Lived Time of Nationhood' – which was first published in *Radical Notes* on April 1, 2008, and which subsequently appeared as the first monograph in the Radical Notes book/booklet series being brought out by Aakar Books – together with 'Kafka and the Question of Revolutionary Subjectivity' (*Radical Notes*, March 13, 2009), 'Media and the State' (*Radical Notes*, December 27, 2006) and 'The Blind Art of the Concrete' (a short review note written in response to a retrospective of the visually challenged Bengal School doyen, Benodebehari Mukherjee, in February 2007), constitute a constellation produced through such a critical, politico-ethical practice of cultural theory.

The three essays that follow – 'In Defence of Hamas' (*Radical Notes*, January 11, 2009), 'Sri Lanka: Genocide and Other Majoritarian Falsehoods' (*Radical Notes*, February 9, 2009) and 'Fascism in its Liberal Womb' (*Radical Notes*, November 18, 2008)—seek to locate the logic of class in movements and politics waged in the idioms of religious, ethno-nationalist and/or ethno-religious identity. In that process, they attempt to capture the objective logic of formation of those identities, and separate them from how those identities are subjectively articulated by its bearers. As a consequence, radical ethno-religious and chauvinist-nationalist identities—such as that of the Palestinian Hamas and the Sri Lankan Tamil LTTE respectively—are found articulating the working-class tendency of critical autonomy in the determinate specificity of their respective spatio-temporal locations by virtue of their objective location. It is in those terms of the (class) logic of formation and orientation that even the religious fundamentalism of Muslims on the Indian subcontinent are distinguished from the apparently similar communalism of the Hindus. In fact, even the traditional, a priori binary between good secularism and bad religiosity is sought to be reversed ('In Defence of Hamas' and 'Fascism in its Liberal Womb') in terms of their constitutive class logic of objective production and/or positioning. Such a theoretical move, which seeks to locate movements and aspirations that are geographically and culturally distant in the objectivity of their formational logic of critical autonomy, is vital because it helps us envisage our politics and aspirations as internal to theirs in terms of the essence of class.

That, however, is never an excuse to turn crudely objectivist. The essays critique, either implicitly or explicitly, the identitarian subjectivity of the bearers of identities—which have been objectively constituted by the working-class logic of critical autonomy—for failing to self-reflexively grasp in their subjectivity the objective logic of the formation of their identities. This is the reason why these movements remain localist and "economistic", and, in the ultimate analysis, turn reactionary.

The last two essays —'Lalgarh Beyond Maoism, Maoism Beyond Lalgarh' (*Radical Notes*, June 24, 2009) and 'Three Fragmentary Theses on the Politico-theoretical Problematic posed by the Current Phase of the Indian Maoist Movement for Working Class Politics' (*Radical Notes*, December 24, 2009)—seek to underscore the fleeting appearance of self-reflexivity within the Maoist movement, and then criticise it for not being able to hold on to this self-reflexivity. The two essays critique the Maoist movement for conflating the discursivity of its localised form of politics with the universal logic of critical autonomy that has been the impulse of formation of its political form in the determinateness of its locality. Such absence of self-reflexivity, which is doubtless not the bane of supposed identitarian movements alone, has ensured that the culture (form) of Maoist politics in India becomes a discursivised articulation of its form. The class logic of such politics, which does not grasp its form in terms of the universal logic of critical autonomy that impelled its determinate formation, is bourgeois. At any rate, it is articulated by the hegemonic logic of capital. That has prevented the generalisation of the formational logic of the Maoist movement beyond the specificity of its locality of emergence as the determinate expression of that proletarian logic of critique of political economy. But the critical acknowledgement of this gap between the determinate objectivity of the movement and the subjective, over-generalised centering of its form in all its discursive and sectarian glory is, I hope, the beginning of the process of determinate generalisation of the revolutionary, counter-discursive proletarian subjectivity through and across various discursivised junctures of capital-labour contradiction.

The principal impulse of the essays here is to negate the discursivity of various existing political forms and politico-intellectual formations that, because of such formalised discursivity, render the expression of autonomy impossible. Some of the essays do, however, seek to go beyond that negationist dimension of critique to express and assert, in an almost Mallarmean poetic act of anti-philosophical expressionism, the various enunciations of autonomy determinate to the specificity of their respective junctures. And yet, what, for the most part, is lacking in these essays is the delineation and explication of the concept of autonomy that is either sought to be wrenched from the repressive discursiveness of different political-ideological forms and politico-intellectual formations through their negation, or plainly asserted as the forms in and through which such autonomy expresses itself specific to various determinate moments of domination and repression. This autonomy, considering that it is constantly sought to be expressed and asserted through the negation of various forms and their concomitant regimes of discursivity, can only be conceptualised as a counter-discursive singularity whose *immanence* is *expressed* because the existence of *immanence* as *immanence* can only be *critical-relational* to the horizon of alienation, duality and discursiveness which preclude such counter-discursive singularity and unalienated immanence. This affirmative conceptualisation of autonomy as a critically positioned, counter-discursive singularity can, following Alain Badiou, be given the common name of "the event". In this affirmative conceptual explication of the event is included the negationist dimension of critique, which in turn implies the condition of possibility of the counter-discursive singularity in its determinateness. In terms of our concern here with the relationship between culture and class, the event can be conceptualised as the emergence of a culture (form), which in and through its enunciative eruption, articulates critical autonomy or rupture vis-à-vis a representative horizon of forms and its logic of discursivity and duality.

This affirmative conceptualisation of the critical counter-discursive singularity, or event, in terms of either its various assertive/expressive phenomenologies or negationist moves is crucial. For, in the absence of such an affirmative conceptualisation, the theoretical project articulated by the thematic unity of these 13 essays cannot be grounded in the politics of class with exacting scrupulousness. That would be so because without the rigour of a philosophy for (not of) the event—wherein the philosophical concept does not have a regulative, truth-producing ontological status but is a "truth-procedure" (Badiou) that enables the constant reclamation of the logic of critical counter-discursive singularity amid concrete historical contradictions—the immanence of rupture in moments of crisis can never be grasped and actualised. And this truth-procedure, in the context of the problematic posed by this book, would be cultural forms or ontologies that self-reflexively grasp their logic of evental formation and posit themselves in those terms. My conceptualisation of the insurgent metaphor, I believe, bears a strong methodological affinity to Badiou's concept of the truth-procedure.

Most of the essays, given that they were formulated as theoretical responses to immediate problems in the realm of political pragmatics, have a pronounced polemical accent. That, needless to say, is the reason behind the rather feeble emphasis on conceptualising the affirmative dimension of critique and autonomy. As a matter of fact, polemics constitute the singular preoccupation and tenor of the *Correspondence* and *New Correspondence* essays that are chronologically older. But a deliberate movement towards affirmative conceptual explication becomes more clearly visible in the later essays, which first appeared in *Radical Notes*. The polemical/negationist orientation remains, nevertheless, the salient feature of all the essays here. My plea to the readers would, however, be to discern in this heavy polemical accent the affirmative part of the negative that is implied by the negationist orientation and register of polemics. This ought not to be construed as an appeal to paper over the absence of rigour, though. It should, instead, be treated as an appeal to see the book as a text that opens up a theoretical project, whose continued deepening would be constitutive of the rhizomatic development of working-class revolutionary politics on the Indian subcontinent.

That I should have chosen the form of the fragmentary essay to articulate a thematic unity that is this book is not an accidental paradox. I have followed Walter Benjamin, particularly the Benjamin of the 'Epistemo-Critical Prologue' of *The Origin of German Tragic Drama*, to envisage fragments as complete autotelic and self-referential-universalities-in-themselves that come into being determinately in a critically inverse relationship to the representative and thus externalised determination of a discursive and dualising system. A fragment, therefore, is the trace of the total that has both occurred and will occur again, and in occurring over and over again will keep constituting the total both in its various finite localities and in its infinite totality. The thematic thread that weaves these essays together into an essential unity is precisely the logic or condition of their possible existence as such critically autonomous events in the disparate determinateness of their respective historical moments. Benjamin writes, "Tirelessly the process of thinking makes new beginnings, returning in a roundabout way to its original object. This continual pausing for breath is the mode most proper to the process of contemplation. For by pursuing different levels of meaning in its examination of one single object it receives both the incentive to begin again and the justification for its irregular rhythm." It is for this reason alone that these essays, which "pursue different (determinate) levels of meaning in their examination of one single object" of the logic of counter-discursive singularity or autonomy, are "essays *in*", and not *on*, "culture and class".

It is, in fact, for this very reason that the sequence of the essays in the book follow, not the chronological order in which they first appeared, but an order that articulates a certain trajectory of unfolding and development of a theme that is unabashedly post-facto. The book, insofar as it is the embodiment of this theme, is the beginning and anticipation of, as I have mentioned earlier, a project of *open* revolutionary praxis.

1

In Search of Class

Ever since the Soviet iron-curtain was shredded and the Tiananmen uprising exposed the chinks in the Chinese model of socialism, a mutation, that was slowly but silently going on in the depths of the political consciousness of the Left, since World War II, suddenly started becoming more pronounced. Class, that historical cornerstone of proletarian politics, has been going into a kind of freeze and has acquired the status of a fetishised divinity. It has become the Holy Grail, which today attracts no more than continual lip service from the phrase-mongering communistological clergy who don the cassocks of 'revolution'.

And though this has largely been true for the Left the world over, it is here on the subcontinent that the phenomenon has, unfortunately enough, been most in evidence. Class, contrary to being a salient feature of an authentic Marxist discourse that grapples with the human being as a species in historical motion is today no more than an heirloom, meant to be prominently showcased in the museum of working-class political history.

Thus the category, which according to Althusser, had broken with its essentialised subjectivity in 'Early Marx's' Feuerbachian scheme to become a different "modality of reflection"—something that transformed material history while simultaneously being transformed by it—has once again been returning to its pre-Marxian past. Althusser (1996, pp. 46-47) writes: "If it is true that Marx espoused a whole problematic, then his rupture with Feuerbach..., implied the adoption of a *new problematic* which even if it did integrate a certain number of the old concepts, did so into a whole which confers on them a radically new significance. I am pleased to be able to express this in an image from Greek history which Marx himself used: after serious set-backs in the War against the Persians, Themistocles advised the Athenians to leave the land and base the future of their city *on another element*—the sea. Marx's theoretical revolution was precisely to base his theory *on a new element* after liberating it from its *old element*: the element of Hegelian and Feuerbachian philosophy." (Emphases author's).

Sadly, what could be considered one of the cardinal axioms of Marxist science has completely eluded the Indian Left, including our putative communists. Class for them is not the "*new element*" Marx had meant it to be. And if we go by the politico-ideological practices of the Indian Left over the past five decades, we discover that class in the Left's discourse has failed to retain the historical connotation Marx had loaded it with. Today, class is no longer a dynamic social category that keeps renewing itself in a process of historical-material becoming by unlocking the critical energies immanent in every moment of historical motion. It is, ironically enough, a sociologised concept harking back to the post-Industrial Revolutionary universe of 18th-19th century Europe; a positive ontology among many others. These varying ontologies (or subjectivities)—which are held together by the hierarchical rules of some sort of a social contract into a stable and supposedly stabilising civil society—are reified moments of the process of historical becoming that are abstracted and alienated from one another, thanks to the fundamentally competitive ethic of capital. It is this ideological impulse—which has permeated all the nooks and crannies of human existence with the ascendancy of capitalism—that has disrupted the non-identitarian flow of a pre-capitalist order by territorialising the various spatio-temporal moments of the flow and freezing them into identities. It is only through deterritorialisation of these separate identities and their respective forms that the non-identitarian, non-alienated whole can be reconstituted.

The mere adding up of these identities does not make that whole. The whole, as Hegel would have said, is more than a sum of its parts. For, the parts have to collapse into one another, and their identities consequently dissolved, for the whole to emerge. And that is precisely the kind of operation the classical Marxist idea of class is meant to perform by historicising the abstracted or reified spatio-temporal moments or identities of the non-identitarian flow. In other words, each identity has to be seen as a moment or a node in the process and thus dissolved or de-reified and made part of that process. In real terms, this implies that two or more different identities and their contradictions have to be seen as they concretely arose due to a certain direction taken by the unfolding of history because of contingent material reasons. That is, unravel the historical-material causes behind the birth of these identities through their separation and alienation from each other, ultimately leading to their antagonisms, hierarchies, competition and contradictions. And once this historicising operation takes place, they are dialectically collapsed into one another. Had this been limited to the realm of speculative philosophy and idealism, we could have safely concluded that the whole had once again been reconstituted. But we live in flesh and blood, and amid concrete history. And things here are not so simple. The moment this operation is over and the identities are dialectically reconciled, giving rise to what ought to have been the higher, non-identitarian whole, which holds its lower halves within itself in a sublated form, it becomes another identity struggling with its antitheses—which are not merely new contradictory identities that have emerged to compete with it, but also include lower forms that it holds within itself, and which now seek to struggle against it, too. As a result, this synthesis, this supposed whole, becomes another new form or identity in the jungle of forms or identities.

This historicising process, therefore, has to go on forever. Certainly, as long as the capitalist mode of production survives. And it can halt at its own peril in a Marxological telos of either a 'fully-formed' communist party or a 'post-revolutionary' society that are eternal. One has to bear in mind the fact that as long the capitalist mode of production lives, all historicising endeavours will finally end up creating newer and newer identities. And that is because the fundamental impulse of capitalism is competition, which is enabled only through the stagnation of the non-identitarian process of becoming into congealed identities that are alienated parts of the whole; or abstracted moments in the process of becoming. Thus all identities, subjectivities or forms need to be continuously critiqued, in a discursive ensemble of theory and practice. And this continuous critique, for a Marxist, unfolds by constantly trying to go beyond the positive. That is, the revolutionary gaze of Marxism has to always delve into the heart of a subjectivity or identity and see not what it shows but what it conceals! It has to always try and transcend the metaphysical present—the a priori identities—by traveling through and heightening their apparent contradictions, only to dissolve them into the historical process from which they were abstracted or reified. This reification of subjectivities or identities can actually be likened to the process of forgetting. An identity forgets, kind of, the process from which it arose. A revolutionary Marxist's task is to make it remember its history and rid itself of its alienation and thus its *identified* existence. This *negative dialectics* is what class consciousness, according to Marx, is all about.

In the absence or slackening of such consciousness or praxis, history is transformed into a static entity, which is then recognised as such by the false consciousness of positive bourgeois existence that has a dialectical co-determining relationship with what Althusser called the ideological state apparatuses. As a consequence, the bourgeois social order, civil society in respectable parlance of the day, is premised on this synchronising and reifying impulse of competitive and, thus, hierarchical capitalism. This is essential to the existence, continuance, expansion and intensification of capitalist processes. In short, the social formation known as the civil society—a hierarchical organisation of various subjectivities—is basically nothing more than a kind of concatenation of production relations essential and intrinsic to the capitalist mode of production. And these production relations, according to Althusser, have to be reproduced if capitalism has to survive. He (1971, pp. 132-133) writes: "However, it is not enough to ensure for labour power the material conditions of its reproduction if it is to be reproduced as labour power. I have said that the available labour power must be 'competent', i.e. suitable to be set to work in the complex system of the process of production. The development of the productive forces and the type of unity historically constitutive of the productive forces at a given moment produce the result that the labour power has to be (diversely) skilled and therefore reproduced as such. Diversely: according to the requirements of the socio-technical division of labour, its different 'jobs' and 'posts'....

> "To put it more scientifically, I shall say that the reproduction of labour power requires not only a reproduction of its skills, but also, at the same time, a reproduction of its submission to the rules of the established order, i.e. a reproduction of submission to the ruling ideology for the workers, and a reproduction of the ability to manipulate the ruling ideology correctly for the agents of exploitation and repression, so that they, too, will provide for the domination of the ruling class 'in words'....
>
> "The reproduction of labour power thus reveals as its *sine qua non* not only the reproduction of it 'skills' but also the reproduction of its subjection to the ruling ideology or of the 'practice' of that ideology, with the proviso that it is not enough to say 'not only but also', for it is clear that *it is in the forms and under the forms of ideological subjection that provision is made for the reproduction of the skills of labour power.*" (Emphases author's.)

But the constitution of the social formation and the ideological apparatuses, which perpetuate it while simultaneously being its parts, are intimately linked to the capitalist mode of production. As a result, any revolutionary subjectivity, the moment it loses its negative-critical continuity, is deprived of its radical sting and is transformed into a reified, ideologised subjectivity that fits into the civil society and becomes its part. In fact, that is how capital has often adapted to the critique of revolutionary praxis, by reifying the revolutionary process into a hardened 'revolutionary' subjectivity. And history testifies how this has contaminated many effective revolutionary endeavours. Stalin's USSR, China's current model of market socialism and the sorry state of affairs as far as the Indian Left goes are but a few instances of the ideologising power of capitalism.

This is the lesson Marx, by pointing to the principal contradiction between capital and labour, intended to impart. And the category of class that he employed is meant to perform precisely that function: discerning the historical-material processes from which contradictory and competing identities are abstracted and in the same revolutionary subjective moment collapse them dialectically to inject motion back into "prehistory" (history with a false consciousness) and transform it into "real history" of non-identitarian becoming, where the reign of exchange value is replaced by the world of use value. Marx, however, was a product of his times—19th century industrial Europe—and obviously his idea of class was delimited by his history. Fredric Jameson (1996, p. 6) hits the nail on its head when he writes: "All science... projects not just ideology but a host of possible ideologies, and this is to be understood in a positive sense: ideology as the working theory of a specific practice, the latter's 'philosophy' as it were, and the ensemble of values and visions that mobilise it and lend it an ethic and a politics (and an aesthetic as well). The various Marxisms—for there are many of them, and famously incompatible with one another—are just that: the local ideologies of Marxian science in history and in concrete historical situations, which set not merely their priorities but also their limits." And this ought to have applied to Marx's Marxism before anybody else's. It ought to have enabled the bearers of his legacy to see the historical correlate of class for Marx was the capitalist and the worker. In such a scenario, it would be fundamentally and gravely erroneous to read him, particularly *Capital*, only historically. That fallacy, nevertheless, has time and again wormed its way into the heart and soul of Marxian revolutionary theory and practice. What has to be extracted from Marx and his historical, and ideological, concept of class is not merely its historicity, but something much more crucial: its logicity that is axiomatic and, therefore, constitutes it as the science of historical materialism. The failure of the Indian left on that count compels it to envisage class, even now, in the same Industrial Revolutionary terms in which Marx had formulated it. As if there has been no intensification of capitalist processes since Marx, and more formal and real subsumptive occurrences have not taken place with the penetration of capital into zones that were still relatively less commodified in Marx's day. So, class for the Indian Left has actually become no more than a sociological descriptor of the western society in the heyday of Industrial Revolution. Unsurprisingly, therefore, working class as envisaged by the Indian Left is an economistic, workerist subjectivity that fits perfectly well into the capitalist social formation and serves it fine. Its only contribution to working-class struggles has been to nurture an entrenched labour aristocracy. Marx (1976, p. 617) states in his ninth thesis on Feuerbach: "The highest point reached by contemplative materialism, that is, materialism which does not comprehend sensuousness as practical activity, is the contemplation of single individuals and of civil society." So, if the subjectivity of the working class, as envisaged by Marx in a certain historical frame, is not seen as arising from its "sensuous experience", which in turn is linked to its "practical activity", it will fail to historically transform itself and become a reified component of the civil society.

It is this debility of the Left that has led to the liquidationist canker, which is slowly gnawing away at its revolutionary soul. Consequently, class, for the Indian Left, has become a piece of immovable liability that most of them secretly desire would disappear, so that they can then proceed to conduct their anti-systemic politics of 'real democratisation' with no qualms. It has been entirely due to the Left's inability to see identity-formation—race, caste, or community—and their concomitant politics in terms of capitalist subsumption and its competitive ethic that has led them to confused vacillation between what they understand as class politics and various types of 'democratising' identity politics. This confusion, which has afflicted the Left not merely here, but all over the world, has been responsible for the rise of the twin beasts of postmodernism and post-Marxism.

Once the Marxists failed to establish a connection between the hardening of diffused and syncreticistic pre-capitalist identities into competing and struggling interest groups and the penetration of capital into relatively more non-commodified zones, the petty-bourgeois radicals of yore now donning the new regalia of post-Marxism and postmodernism took over and declared that class was an identity that had become redundant in an era of more pressing identity struggles. In India, such 'pomo' and 'poma' tendencies are articulated by the Subaltern Studies collective, as also by "neo-traditionalists" such as Ashis Nandy. Their desire, not very different from many modernists, who appeared on the European horizon during and after 1848, is to rediscover our unalienated, non-commodified, pre-modern pasts that were thoroughly marginalised, if not destroyed, by modernity borne on the wings of big capital. Sample this excerpt from Nandy (1987, p. xvii): "...modernity is neither the endstate of all cultures nor the final word in institutional creativity. Howsoever formidable and permanent the edifices of the modern world may appear today, the other self recognises, one day there will have to be post-modern societies and a post-modern consciousness, and those societies and that consciousness may choose to build not so much upon modernity as on the traditions of the non-modern or pre-modern world." What they don't realise is that their discourses of non-alienation and their politics of anti-capitalism and critique of modernity are articulated by the competitive ethic of capitalism itself. Their non-commodified, pre-modern Weltanschauung is a subjectivity that has to compete with and struggle against capitalism, commodification and modernity. In that sense, their whole discourse, despite its purported critique of modernity, is *modern*.

And such ideological discourses share a paradigm not merely with the apparently progressive identity politics articulated by Gandhians and sundry civil rights activists such as Medha Patkar, Vandana Shiva, et al, but also with casteist forces like the BSP and SP, and even the fascists of the Sangh parivar. Not surprisingly, varying and often mutually oppositional political forces—the tribal outfits in the Northeast and ethno-religious separatists of Kashmir—inhabit the same ideological space. The Left parties, not knowing what to do in such a scenario, have been swinging wildly between berating such "anti-class" tendencies and then adopting their piecemeal politics by attaching labels such as the 'People's Democratic Revolution', the 'National Democratic Revolution' and the 'New Democratic Revolution' on to them. They have often enough even aligned with them. Various Marxist-Leninist outfits have limited themselves to giving leadership to tribal identity politics in Bastar, Telangana, Jharkhand, West Bengal and Orissa. The repeated entente of the official Left—the CPI and the CPI (M)—with caste and regional-linguistic political forces against the Hindutva of the Sangh parivar is only an indication of the Fascist conjuncture in which we are and the complete ideological blindness of the Left to the problem.

This blindness manifests in many ways. The most notable has been the Left's recent ambivalence on the Islamist ummah of Osama bin Laden vis-a-vis the imperialist US. Probably, the various Left parties vest their anti-imperialist hope in Al Qaeda. Indian communist parties have often come so close to extolling the anti-imperialist virtues of a force such as Al Qaeda that it has chosen to overlook the historical-theoretical formulations of world Marxism that reactionary, petty-bourgeois anti-capitalism is something that emerges from the political-economic womb of capitalism to further reinforce it. For instance, one of the key CPI-ML groups had, during the US-led invasion of Iraq, chosen to conflate their defence of Iraqi sovereignty against its arbitrary and unconscionable violation with a stout and spirited defence of Saddam Hussein. The group had gone to the extent of upholding Saddam against the Bush-Blair imperialist phalanx, and making a hero out of this anti-Marxist, Baathist criminal. Little do they realise that nation-states can hardly be units of anti-imperialism and that, in fact, the constitutive tendency of free competition among nation-states is the increasing monopoly of capitalism as a system, which is precisely what is described as imperialism in politico-ideological terms.

The struggle against imperialism has to be finally a struggle against capitalism in its various forms—both that of Bush and Blair, as also that of Saddam and Bin Laden. The hegemony of global capitalism has to be critiqued simultaneously with the *swadeshiism*[1] of the fascists and custodians of national capital who uphold the virtues of the Indian nation-state apparently against global capitalist onslaughts from the West. And the communal Hindutva of the Sangh parivar has to be resisted as much as the kulak-based caste identity politics of Lalu Yadav or petty-bourgeois politics of Dalitism a la Mayawati.

In short, Indian Marxists need to turn sensitive to the dialectical linkages between capitalism and petty-bourgeois anti-capitalism. After all, it was not for nothing that Henri Lefebvre (1991) claimed Fascism to be a mystification of the revolution? Petty-bourgeois opposition to the alienation wrought by capital's penetration into relatively less commodified areas and zones of simple commodity production is what leads to the constitution of a Fascist conjuncture—with Bonapartist and Fascist forces ranged against or with each other—because petty bourgeois subjectivities of caste, community, race, language and region are the result of capitalist subsumption and competition. They in their reified anti-capitalism and for their supposed politics of non-alienation enable capital accumulation to overcome its crisis by expropriation of the commons and social means of the production.

The Indian Marxists, if they really wish to fight Fascism—its shadow looms large on the subcontinent—will have to realise soon enough that Marx's notion of class has to be made historical through what John S. Saul (2003) calls "classifying of difference". This means that the subjectivity of class has to continuously change and it can do so by constantly and dialectically superseding the identity-based differences that will keep cropping up as long as there is even a minute trace of capitalism left in the world. Therefore, in the ultimate analysis, this classifying of difference is nothing else but a call to, what Marx had termed, "revolution in permanence"!

NOTE

1. Swadeshiism is an idea that was originally conceived and used by Mahatma Gandhi during the Indian freedom struggle. It was meant to champion the cause of products, particularly cloth produced by weavers in India, and the boycott of British goods. It has now been adopted by a wing of the RSS—the Swadeshi Jagran Manch—to fight 'western imperialism'.

REFERENCES

Althusser, Louis, 'Feuerbach's 'Philosophical Manifestoes''. In *For Marx*, tr. Ben Brewster (Verso, London, 1996)

Althusser, Louis, 'Ideology and Ideological State Apparatuses'. In *Lenin and Philosophy and Other Essays*, tr. Ben Brewster (Monthly Review Press, New York, 1971)

Jameson, Fredric, *Late Marxism* (Verso, London, 1996)

Lefebvre, Henri, *Critique of Everyday Life*, Vol. 1, tr. John Moore (Verso, London, 1991)

Marx, Karl, 'Theses on Feuerbach'. In Karl Marx and Fredrick Engels, *The German Ideology* (Progress Publishers, Moscow, 1976)

Nandy, Ashis, 'Preface'. In *Traditions, Tyranny, and Utopias* (Oxford University Press, New Delhi, 1987)

Saul, John S. 'Identifying Class, Classifying Difference'. In *Fighting Identities: Race Religion and Ethnonationalism; Socialist Register 2003*. Edited by Leo Panitch and Colin Leys (K.P. Bagchi & Company, Kolkata, 2003)

2

Fascism and a Marxist Praxis of Art

> "Mankind, which in Homer's time was an object of contemplation of the Olympian gods, now is one for itself. Its self-alienation has reached such a degree that it can experience its own destruction as an aesthetic pleasure of the first order. This is the situation of politics which Fascism is rendering aesthetic. Communism responds by politicizing art."
>
> —Water Benjamin, 'The Work of Art in the Age of Mechanical Reproduction' (*Illuminations*, tr. Harry Zohn [Fontana, 1992], p. 235)

The highest form of aestheticised politics, to cite Benjamin (1995, pp. 234-235) once again, is war. And don't we know that well enough! The belligerence on our borders with Pakistan, the Indian army well turned-out in its menacing regalia with its array of ordered and sophisticated weaponry. That is the beauty of militarised order, something the khaki shorts of the RSS brilliantly embody in the domain of both civil and political societies. There is but a thin line that separates Praveen Togadia's *trishul diksha*, and the orderly, disciplined and 'aesthetic' drill at the *shakhas* and the Saraswati Shishu Mandirs, from the orchestrated and organised *danse macabre* of the Bajrangi and Sanghi death squads on the streets of Gujarat, post Godhra. It is this fascist spirit—of its obsession with aesthetic beauty, going to the extent of aestheticising its violent credo—that was so tellingly captured by Leni Riefenstahl's 'artistic' films, which relied heavily on the footage of the militarised, and murderous Nazi order on German streets.

There might have been some let-up, at least apparently, in the unabated ascendancy of the Hindu Right of late, but that is perhaps because its fascist credentials, particularly with regard to its typical politics-aesthetics kinship, has got generalised into an ideology that pervades and articulates our neo-liberal society and polity in their entirety. That is precisely the reason why practising Marxists need to urgently intervene and discover what aesthetic sensibilities are all about.

Fascism, as a form of bourgeois regime, thrives on the synchrony the state power of the big bourgeoisie achieves with the petty-bourgeois fascistic tendencies present in a socio-political order where various forms and stages of capitalism coexist. Consequently, violence remains no longer merely a function of the repressive state apparatus (Althusser 1971, p. 137), but extends itself into the domain of ideology and 'civil society'. For, violence and repression are integral to the various petty-bourgeois ideological structures: caste, ethnicity, race, religion, et al. This movement of violence from the domain of state power to that of the 'civil society' is dialectical and the other half of this dialectic is the ideologisation of polity. Put simply, polity, essentially constituted by the various repressive state apparatuses, is seen as an extension of the ideologised realm of 'civil society' and not as someting that exists independent of and outside it. Surprisingly, this is precisely what the Marxists would want. Unfortunately, for them, this collapse of the state on to the sphere of ideology is marshalled by the fascists, not to foster revolutionary stirrings, but to consolidate the power of the state and its ruling classes. There is, of course, a difference in how Marxists perceive this state/'civil society' synergy and how the Fascists would want people to visualise it. While for the former 'civil society' is the domain where the coercive state power of the ruling elite is complemented by its consent-generating ideologies and is thus also a realm of class struggle; for the latter, the state is only an instrument to purportedly carry forward the will of a *majoritarionised* 'civil society' split along petty-bourgeois ideological lines of religion, caste, race, ethnicity, etc.

This perhaps explains how a fascist regime generates consensus for its politics. Not only that, it also indicates how such a regime is contingent on—in fact, derives its power from—the absolute congealment of ideological mores and values already existing in 'civil society'. It is precisely at this juncture that we need to understand that art in its current forms, since it is practised in the domain of 'civil society' and is constitutive of it, has bourgeois ideological moorings. 'Civil society', as we see above, is the realm where the political rule of capital and its various classes extends itself through its apparatuses of consent. Consequently, the ideological grain of aesthetic sensibilities that simultaneously informs and is derived from such artistic practices has to be located if the process of consensus-generation at work, vis-a-vis fascism, is to be correctly pointed out and combated. This, according to Benjamin, is the "politicization of art" and is perhaps the only accurate Marxist response possible in these times of fascist/neo-liberal ascendancy.

To begin at the beginning, we shall try to examine the ideological character of what is commonly perceived as art in our times. In the process, an attempt shall be made to lay bare the reifications inherent in the preponderant aesthetic sensibilities of our times by treating them in historical-materialist terms. Finally, we shall try to come up with a formulation of what artistic practice and aesthetics can mean in terms of Marxist praxis in a fascist conjuncture. What, however, needs to be clarified is that the attempt here is to only draw up a general and tentative theoretical outline of a Marxist approach to aesthetics. Therefore, the essay, though alluding to certain Indian artistic and literary practices germane to its various contentions, will not focus primarily on Indian artistic practices, vis-a-vis the fascist gestures of the Hindu Right.

The Ideology of Modern Art

It is absolutely imperative that we locate the ideology of the aesthetic sensibility currently in vogue, if we are to comprehend how the perceptual field of the common citizenry, under the influence of fascism, imputes 'beauty' to war and militarised discipline, thus consenting to its reactionary and dangerous politics. The uncovering of the ideological origins of art as it has come to be understood in its post-Renaissance, post-Enlightenment modern sense will presumably shed some light on how people who watch fascist displays of violence, war and militarisation from a distance, can be made to aestheticise them and, consequently, become a part of its political project.

This exercise will also arguably reveal why and how art, in its current liberal forms, is ultimately ineffectual in fighting fascism. The burden of my argument being that the latter draws its sustenance from the ideological premises of passive consumption and 'classless' individuals comprising an equally 'classless' 'civil society'. Premises that are fundamentally crucial to the survival and existence of contemporary art too. However, in order to proceed further with this theorisation, it is important to get a historical fix on how these notions of the 'classless' individual, 'civil society' and passive consumption came into being. It is also equally important that we realise the links between these notions and the gaze of modern art, which is at the basis of both its production and accessing. To talk in historical-materialist terms, we need to locate the origin of these ideas in their specific conjuncture. Only that will enable us to unearth their ideological field.

Art, as we know it today, is largely the production of individuals. Other individuals access the works of art thus produced. Even in case of modern theatre, cinema or performances of some forms of western classical or popular music—supposed to be collective endeavours—it is the director or the conductor, or the bandleader whose view of how the movie or the play or the musical performance is to play itself out, guides the whole effort. So, even though such productions are apparently the consequence of a collective effort, the individuals participating in it interact with each other within a hierarchised field presided over by the leader of the team (the director, conductor, etc.). Thus, hierarchy delimits the role each individual can play with regard to the final product. For instance, the editor, cinematographer, music director screenplay writer and so on, in case of a film, have to work in accordance with the directives of the filmmaker, who is their absolute superior. In such circumstances, a film is, first and foremost, the director's product. In case of music, the performers' role is subordinate to that of the composer's, before all else, and then the conductor's. Of course, the star principle, which has been the natural consequence of what we identify as art today and which has resulted in the emergence of the art mart, has, in most cases, led to the privileging of the performers (thanks to their visibility) over the 'actual' producers (filmmakers, composers, conductors.). For now, though, it would suffice to state that the ethic of individuated production, which dominates even supposedly collective artistic enterprises like cinema and theatre, is borne out by their individuated and passive consumption. The audience, though it is apparently a collective, accesses the film or the play, not together as a whole unit, but as individuals. As a result, such an audience is only capable of passively taking in the productions put before it; its members do not actively participate in the production process itself. For collective accessing of artistic productions to occur, it is not enough to sit together in the same auditorium and watch a film, a play or a concert.

What needs to be elucidated at this point is the 'ideology of the individual' because only by elaborating upon that will we be able to grasp the provenance and principles of what is commonly perceived as art. This individual, whose ethics of individuality constitute the origins of modern art, is defined in opposition to a reality that is external to him. What this, in effect, means is he contemplates a reality that is separate from his being. Obviously, therefore, the individual and his subjectivity are not part of that reality and the reality that he gazes upon is alien to his being. Art, in its current modern form, is contingent on this conception of the individual alienated and separate from reality. It is thus the individual subject's representation of how he has contemplated a reality external to him. It is, therefore, no accident that all art, which is self-conscious of its modern sense, is autographed, emphasising the fact that it is the production of an individual. The ethic of individuated production and the consequent split between the producer and the consumer are not more than six centuries old. The perception of art in its modern form goes on to prove that it is a product of a particular mode of production. The producer-consumer split that lies at the heart of modern art also goes on to show that the mode of production within which works of contemporary art are produced and consumed is capitalist. As a result, art in its modern sense is a commodity.

But aren't modern works of art, premised as they are on the 'birth of the individual and a reality external to him', ideological? To put it more clearly, isn't the individual, the way we have encountered him above, an ideology? And if that is so, isn't the modern art product an ideology too? The answers to all these questions are in the affirmative. And that is precisely the source of a little confusion. Ideology, according to Althusser (1971), enables the perpetuation, expansion and intensification of a social formation that arises from a specific mode of production by reproducing the social relations of production that constitute the social formation in question. So, if modern art, with the conception of the contemplative individual at its heart, is an ideology, how can it also be a commodity—a product produced within a mode of production? In other words, how can an ideology (modern art), which is meant to perpetuate a socio-economic formation of a mode of production, be a product that is produced within the same mode of production? This contradiction is, however, only an apparent one that can be resolved if we are able to perceive a more nuanced and dialectical relationship at work between ideologies and modes of production.

Ideologies are disseminated and accessed through what Althusser (1971, pp. 131-133) calls ideological state apparatuses. In fact, ideological state apparatuses, which facilitate the dissemination and accessing of ideologies, cannot be different from channels that enable the distribution of products produced by its mode of production. The channels of distribution are integral to and define a mode of production. And since the products of contemporary art are consumed passively as commodities, the mode of production within which they are produced is the capitalist mode of production. In short, modern art products are accessed as bourgeois ideologies precisely because they are produced to be consumed as commodities—products of the capitalist mode of production.

Benjamin (1986, p. 222) provides us with an extremely clear formulation of this dialectical relationship between ideas (read ideologies) and their modes of production: In his 'The Author as Producer', he writes:

> "Instead of asking, 'What is the *attitude* of a work to the relations of production of its time? Does it accept them, is it reactionary—or does it aim at overthrowing them, is it revolutionary?'—instead of this question, or at any rate before it, I should like to propose another. Rather than ask, 'What is the attitude of a work to the relations of production of its time?' I should like to ask; 'What is its *position* in them?' This question directly concerns the function the work has within the literary relations of production of its time. It is concerned, in other words, directly with the literary *technique* of works." (Emphases author's.)

Thus, if we take Benjamin's word for it, the "attitude" of works of modern art to the "relations of production (capitalist) of their time", is determined by "their position in them". These works, created by individual producers, who have their 'recognisable' individual styles or voices stamped on their works, can easily be said to have a positive ideological attitude towards the capitalist relations of production—even when they apparently set out to critique capitalism and its ideologies—and the contingent socio-economic formation. This is further clarified if we analyse the "technique" of works of art. Benjamin (1986, p. 222) points out: "In bringing up technique, I have named the concept that makes literary products directly accessible to a social, and therefore a materialist analysis." The social and materialist analysis of the techniques of individuated production of modern art yields, for Benjamin (1986, p. 224), the following conclusion:

> "There were not always novels in the past, and there will not always have to be; not always tragedies, not always great epics; not always were the forms of commentary, translation, indeed, even so-called plagiarism, playthings in the margins of literature; they had a place not only in the philosophical but also in the literary writings of Arabia and China. Rhetoric has not always been a minor form, but set its stamp in antiquity on large provinces of literature."

This goes on to shown that modern art forms and genres, autographed to emphasise their individuated mode of production and their commodified nature have not always been around. Bakhtin (1981), therefore, is not off the mark when he says that autographed literature is but a drop in the vast ocean of oral literatures. Consequently, we can also deduce from this social and materialist analysis that the sense of the representational, which is so overriding in modern art, has its provenance in a certain specific historical moment. The conception that the individual subject is only capable of representing a reality, not participate in actively making it, since it is alienated from him, is what constitutes modern art. A historical-materialist survey of 'artistic' modes—even those which pre-date the rise of modern art and its related aesthetic sensibility and which we perceive as art in a modern aesthetic sense only in retrospect—will, I believe, show that modern art and aesthetic sensibilities have been preceded by various other discourses of reality in which the subject has not always been independent of and/or alienated from his reality. Such discourses of reality articulated a conception of man not alienated from the world and its reality and that what such men created were, for them and their contemporaries, not representations of reality but reality itself. It will also indicate the moment at which the ideology of the individual emerged and the historical-material conditions that led to such an eruption in the history of ideas.

Discourses of Reality: A Dialectical History

For the convenience of our discussion we shall, for now, invert the chronology and begin with the birth of the individual and modern art, and its dialectical interrelationship with the emergence of capitalism. Subsequently, we shall go back in time to conduct a thematically (not methodologically) eclectic investigation to understand what led to this historic rupture. (It is also important to mention as an aside here that the modern aesthetic sensibility, which, arguably, originates in the European Renaissance, had a universalising impact throughout the world [even on the non-western regions], thanks to the spread and expansion of capitalism through the centuries-long process of colonisation.)

The birth of this notion of the individual, and modern art that grew out of it, can be traced back to the European Renaissance, which—according to the consensus that prevails among scholars—began in the 14th century. That the humanised individual, for whom reality was what he saw at the level of his eyes, was a product of the Renaissance was evident in the invention of perspective and the perspectival representation of reality by Renaissance artists. The perspectival view of space, according to Panofsky (1991, p. 27), was integral to the Renaissance and was one in which "the entire picture has been transformed—to cite another Renaissance theoretician—into a 'window,' and...we are meant to believe we are looking through this window into a space". What this effectively means is that the individual human subject looked through a window out into the world and its reality. The perspective revolution of the Renaissance is, therefore, clearly the result of the split between the observer-subject and his observed-reality, and signals the rise of the contemplative individual, a humanised reality, and the representational and individuated ethos of modern art. The perspective revolution and the aesthetic it inaugurated touched literary representations too. Its influence in the realm of literature brought about the birth of the realist and autographed novel with its linear narrative. While the realism of the modern novel can be seen as the reality represented by the perspective of the individual subjectivity of the novelist, the linear narrative symbolises the linearity of time when space acquires depth in a perspectival view of the world.

So overpowering did the ideology of the contemplative individual and his perspectival view of the world become that people, ever since, have accessed all creations—visual, literary and musical—even those that pre-date the Renaissance and its vision of reality, in terms of the modern aesthetic that owes its origins to the Renaissance. The concrete historical-material processes that led to the congealment of this possible vision of humanised reality as a given, in fact, as *reality* itself, were those of the ascendancy and spread of capitalism. The birth of the individual in the age of Renaissance is dialectically linked to the simultaneous coming of age of capitalism and its spirit of individual entrepreneurship in Europe. The period of the European bourgeoisie's incessant struggle against feudalism in Europe and its triumphs is coeval to the Renaissance. One can hardly overstate the universalising politico-ideological triumph of capitalism, considering that all latter-day anti-humanist attempts—Cubism, Dadaism, Surrealism, etc.—to subvert both formally and figuratively the bourgeois aesthetic of perspective, could not rid themselves of the normative presence of the humanising perspective, even though they successfully subverted it at the formal (literal) and even at the figurative level. Ironically, these formal and/or figurative subversions of the perspective were perceived as individual stylistic inventions and breakthroughs. By virtue of being inscribed in the ideological matrix of art, post Renaissance, they were perforce recognised as the productions of individual/s (even if he/she belonged to schools or traditions).

Therefore, to state at this point that the Renaissance, its vision of the contemplative individual and humanised reality—the guiding principles of the modern aesthetic—have been caused by the ascendancy of capitalism would not at all be inaccurate. However, it would definitely be a half-truth that smacked of economic determinism. Since ideologies are products too, they by creating their own processes of production and accessing also give rise to their own modes of intellectual production. Therefore, it can well be argued that bourgeois ideologies of the individual and his humanised reality created their own mode of production (capitalist), and instituted and established it in the larger social order of its time. It also follows from here that the simultaneous development of these ideas and their mode of production would have followed a logic inherent in the structure of Renaissance (and pre-capitalist) socio-economic formations and their ideologies. The Marxian dialectical approach would, however, deal with this problematic at two different conceptual levels. It would first trace the development of an ideology in its internal logical synchronicity and then study it in terms of its historical-materialist diachronicity. Subsequently, it would attempt to integrate the two conceptual explanations dialectically, which would go on to indicate that one does not precede the other but develops together in a simultaneous dynamic.

When the ideology of the individual and his humanised reality is approached in this fashion it reveals that the individual's birth was the result of a rupture in the ideological structure of the pre-Renaissance, pre-capitalist order caused by its own internal logical development. This reconfigured the social formation of its time by establishing the bourgeois mode of production that arose out of this break. While tracing this development, the approach will also indicate that the ascendancy of capitalism and its own unique social relations of production caused the birth of the individual during the Renaissance. Finally, it will integrate these two conceptual halves to show that the ideology of the individual and the Renaissance were as much the products of ascendant capitalism and its sociality, as the latter were caused by the former.

Italian Renaissance artist and author Vasari (1987) has argued that the fundamental reason behind the Renaissance was the inventive talent of its artists. This faculty of invention, according to him, put an end to the repetitiveness of medieval European 'artistic' creations. Vasari, in upholding and celebrating the inventive faculty of the Renaissance artists, underscores their individual subjectivities. From his assertions we can infer that the repetitiveness of the medieval 'artists' signified a fabric of reality of which human beings were an integral part, and individual subjectivities with their individual inventive potential implied the negation of this all-enveloping and continuous fabric of reality. Thus was born the fiercely inventive and contemplative individual who was completely alienated from the reality that surrounded him.

Indologist and Radical Humanist scholar Sibnarayan Ray (2003, p. 39) confirms this when he takes recourse to 18th century French historian Michelet's *La Renaissance* to argue that man, for the first time, discovered the 'outside world' and his 'interior universe' in the 16th century—the heyday of the European Renaissance. This, according to Ray, is evidence of the coming into being of *man* and his *outside world* as two distinct entities. He, with some assistance from the 19th century Swiss historian of Renaissance, Jacob Burckhardt, states: "In the consciousness of the medieval man, the outside world and his inner self were both immersed in a haze of religious beliefs and various kinds of spiritual notions; this man used to see himself as part of the larger creation. In the age of Renaissance, man not only saw the *outside world* for what it was, but also similarly discovered his own *inner self* and through it established his own individuality and was able to work towards its development." (Emphases added.) Now, let us see how Burckhardt (1995, p. 100) himself contrasted the new found anthropocentricism of Renaissance with the Middle Ages:

> "In the Middle Ages both sides of human consciousness—that which was turned within as that which was turned without—lay dreaming or half awake beneath a common veil. The veil was woven of faith, illusion, and childish prepossession, through which the world and history were seen clad in strange hues. Man was conscious of himself only as a member of race, people, party, family, or corporation—only through some general category. In Italy (when Renaissance first started there) this veil first melted into air; an *objective* treatment and consideration of the State and of all the things of this world became possible. The *subjective* side at the same time asserted itself with corresponding emphasis; man became a spiritual *individual*, and recognized himself as such." (Emphases author's.)

But what forced the birth of the contemplative individual? The reply, in terms of diachronicity or the dynamic of history, has been indicated earlier: capitalism's ascendancy vis-a-vis feudalism led to the establishment of the individual that arose from the spirit of individual enterprise and freedom so integral to capitalism and ensured its political supremacy against feudalism's reigning conception of fixed roles in a continuous, though, hierarchised order.

The answer to this question can, however, be complete, only when we have traced its logical synchronic unfolding too. The Renaissance in Europe was preceded by the hierarchised and stratified world of feudalism, with the all-powerful Christian Church ordering its social formation in religious terms. However, there came a time, when some men belonging to the lower strata or stations of this continuous but hierarchised order, and stooping under the burden of its oppression, felt they had to make sense of why their beings, the registers of their discourse and their visions of the world, in spite of being part of the larger fabric of reality and its continuous discourse, were subordinated to the discourses of those who belonged to the upper strata. The yearning to find answers to such questions compelled them to tear themselves off from this continuous, all-pervasive fabric of reality and contemplate it as something distinct from their being, in order to make sense of it and their place in it. This gave rise to the individual for whom reality was what he saw with his *own* eyes and that reality was what this individual could *humanly* make sense of. Russian filmmaker Andrei Tarkovsky, in an eponymous film on the life, times and works of medieval Orthodox Christian monk and icon painter Andrei Rublyev, highlights this process of humanisation. Rublyev's disenchantment with oppressive Russian feudalism of his times and the Orthodox Church's position within it, compels him to conceive of Christ as an ordinary Russian, friend of his poor and suffering fellow-men, which is at variance from how he has been depicted in Churches running under feudal patronage. The passion of this Christ, according to Tarkovsky's Rublyev, was the sacrifice he made for his people. When his humanised view of Christ and Christianity is unable to find a place in the oppressive and barbaric feudal order of his contemporary Russia, Rublyev stops painting icons and takes a vow of silence. He, however, abandons his silence and decides to take up painting again when in the end, he senses the spirit of assertion among the common Russian masses against the oppressive feudal dominance. Tarkovsky's Rublyev symbolises the birth of individual subjectivities and their humanised realities, which played a progressive and emancipatory role in their conjuncture. The point is, how did modern artistic practices, and their individuated mode of production and the resultant process of passive consumption—which emanated from this liberating impulse of contemplative individualism—become an oppressive orthodoxy in another conjuncture. The conjuncture that represents the consolidation of commodity capitalism, with its ideology hegemonising society and its members.

The revolution in the world of ideas during the Renaissance coincided with the peaking of trade, enterprise and capitalism in society at large. The preponderance of monetisation, which the rise of capitalism ensured, gave a fillip to this idea of art and took it to its logical culmination: the market where products of art would be produced by some to be consumed by others as commodities. This was emancipatory as long as it served to free the oppressed from the stratified reign of feudalism. But we also have to comprehend how these once-progressive notions of the contemplative individual and humanisation could come to embody obfuscating false consciousness in another time—that of advanced capitalism and its inegalitarian class rule.

It is, therefore, necessary that we problematise the progressive impulses of the Renaissance, the modern artistic practices coupled with their aesthetics and their historical handmaiden—capitalism—if we are to think and work in terms of an alternative mode of production that is not based on the split between the producer and consumer or the rift between the subject and his reality. For instance, it would be useful to know that the transformation in outlook, brought about by the Renaissance, and its linkages with commodification of ideas and creations, is found in Vasari (1987). This quintessential Renaissance man says the "cognoscenti" will, by their evaluation and appreciation of the artists' creations, effect the artistic 'renaissanceisation' of a society. The general members of that society will have no role to play in this 'renaissanceisation ', except for passively consuming what the artist produce and what the cognoscenti deem fit for them. Therefore, the progressive Renaissance itself, according to one of its key figures, was the result of passive consumption and commodification.

The problematising of these two notions in the realm of art and aesthetics is essential if we are to transcend current artistic practices and aesthetics associated with them, in order to develop a Marxist praxis of art that revolves, not around the alienation between the producer and the consumer, but around the idea of universal production that lays passive consumption, its capitalist socio-economic formation and their ideologies to rest. In so doing, art becomes an inseparable part of Marxist political praxis, the praxis of class struggle.

To proceed in that direction we have to delve deep into the pre-capitalist past of the Renaissance and see for ourselves how various pre-capitalist modes of existence ordered production, production relations and the consequent socio-economic formations. And how these generated their respective modes of interacting with and ordering reality, which gave rise to their own unique ethics of creativity. That the pre-Renaissance worldviews were not centred on the contemplative individual and the humanised reality external to him is clear from our earlier discussion on their origins. In pre-Renaissance feudal Europe, men were not separate or alienated from their reality and were its integral part. However, there was a problem. This discourse of all-pervasive reality, which did not alienate the human subject from its object, was nevertheless a stratified discourse of reality that played a crucial role in preserving and perpetuating feudalism.

Christianity was the matrix of this continuous, unalienated, though stratified, reality of medieval Europe. It was this that occasioned the bourgeois ideology of the free and contemplative individual. The ontological basis of such an individual was his freedom from religion and God—notions that essentially constituted and wove the fabric of this continuous and stratified reality. It can, therefore, be argued that feudalism, despite its stratifications, provided its members with a sense of being part of a larger collective that ordered reality and was in turn ordered by it. The social relations of production that comprised the socio-economic formation of feudalism were, of course, rigidly hierarchised and oppressive, but they provided all its members with some sense of control over the larger production process. This means that men visualised themselves as being one with their reality and not as entities external to it.

Christianity in medieval Europe, or generally religion in any feudal social formation, through the notion of the creator God/s, provided men with this sense of oneness with the larger creation. That is exactly why we shall stop short of labelling religion as generally ideological—the embodiment of false consciousness. In pre-capitalist social formations, religion and the various ways in which its discourse was articulated (icons, statues, paintings, frescoes, chamber music, stories, *kathas, choras, bhajans*, riddles, etc., which we today judge by our post-Renaissance aesthetic standards and consider them as either art or pre-artistic craft), was actually technological. For, it was the organising principle of a cohesive reality made up of unalienated beings. What this means is that the production process was not alienated from the producer men. It implies that men, even those who stood on the lowest rungs (serfs, Dalits and so on) of this hierarchical order, had some kind of control over the large production process and its reality. Religion and God/s were what maintained this rigidly stratified order where the monarch was often the incarnation of God/s on Earth and ruled by some kind of a divine right. By the same logic, the other descending strata were considered representatives (or incarnations) of those above them. Thus even the serf (or the Dalit in case of our Indic civilisation) were, by this account, progeny of God/s, though many times removed. It is this principle of a hierarchical but seamless creation or social order that is reflected in Manu's code where the members of the four varnas—Brahmins, Kshatriyas, Vaishyas and Sudras—are supposed to have originated from various parts of Brahma's (the creator in Indic or Aryanised mythology) body in descending order.

This feudal stratification meant that in the realm of ideas and creativity, various discourses and their different registers too were hierarchised. And though every discourse was supposed to be articulating the reality of creation and participating actively in its making (since even the lowliest of the low was, after all, the progeny of the creator God/s), they were bound together in a superordinate-subordinate relationship that was nevertheless complementary. This contradiction in terms, of complementary hierarchy, meant that the multiplicity of discourses and their registers was present only insofar as lower discourses and their registers were subordinate to and subsumed by those above them. Still, the subject and his/her reality were bound together, inextricably.

This feudal stratification, however, has a prehistory of real complementarity. In primitive human societies, which witnessed the birth of cave and rock-shelter art, every member painted in his or her own way on the walls and ceilings of rock-shelters and caves. But these paintings did not have *individual producers* and all the various individual paintings were, as archaeological and anthropological evidences indicate, seen to be articulating the singular reality of an entire primitive social formation. Anthropologists and archaeologists also conjecture that primitive cave art had religio-magical functions. They sought to explain the elemental experiences of the primitive humans, who were aeons away from being dissociated from their reality. Religion and magic for these primitive human societies, therefore, had no ideological whiff about them. They were purely technological discourses in the sense that they were employed by the primitive human societies to understand the universe and their place in it so that they could work in tandem with it, not on it. For instance, God/s in primitive human societies was the principle that made production possible.

The various cosmogonies were actually languages created to order and apprehend reality and facilitate (its) production. By attributing the creation of the universe to creator God/s, which is exactly what cosmogonies do, they generated a syntax and mode of production. The various forms of cave art, which articulated the technology of religion and magic, could also be considered as some kind of cosmogony, a primitive science. Levi-Strauss (1966, p. 22) writes: "...it is worth showing ...(that) art lies half-way between scientific knowledge and mythical or magical thought." The idea of *bricolage* and *bricoleur* found in Levi-Strauss (1966, pp. 16-17), perhaps, provides the most adequate explanation we can get about primitive human societies and their technology of 'art'. The French anthropologist writes:

> "The 'bricoleur' is adept at performing a large number of diverse tasks; but unlike the engineer, he does not subordinate each of them to the availability of raw materials and tools conceived and procured for the purpose of the project. His universe of instruments is closed and the rules of his game are always to make do with 'whatever is at hand', that is to say with a set of tools and materials which is always finite and is also heterogeneous because what it contains bears no relation to the current project, or indeed to any particular project, but is the contingent result of all the occasions there have been to renew or enrich the stock or to maintain it with the remains of previous constructions or destructions."

Religion or magic, which are accretions around conceptions of good and bad divinities, and demi-gods, constitutes this *bricolage.* The primitive man is, therefore, a *bricoleur,* who is essentially using the extensive, though limited, linguistic repertoire of God/s, religion and magic to produce reality, both in the sense of cave art and myths as also in the sense of what we call necessaries (food, clothing and shelter).

In subsequent pre-feudal social formations, which were the result of a higher degree of sophistication and complexity in terms of their respective modes of production and contingent production relations, there emerged sections or groups of people who provided intellectual, moral and/or political leadership. However, these groups should be considered as some kind of an advanced guard of their time and not permanent headmen. People were mostly elected to these groups by members of the tribes or *janas*—if our focus is on pre-Vedic and Rig Vedic civilisations, or present-day remnants of similarly primitive social formations—and this meant that anybody could aspire to be a part of it and actually move up. The priest, king, Brahmin, *kavi* (poet) or the Indra had no birthright and no one position was absolutely superordinate to the other. Ramvilas Sharma's (1996, pp. 17-21) investigations into the literature of the Vedic period reveal that *kavi* (poet), *rishi* (sage), *vipra, raimbh* and *purohit* were honorifics that were used interchangeably during the Rig Vedic period, that is around 1500 BC. According to both Sharma (1996) and Rahul Sankrityayan (1942), Indra, Agni and other Vedic *devtas* (gods) were not individuals but states, which could be achieved by anyone who had the required qualification. Vashistha, according to Sharma (1996), was the designation for an entire category of sages and not the name of a single sage as it later came to be commonly perceived. Also, the interpretation and making sense of the world was the *kavi* or *rishi's* task and some of their verses in the Rig Veda praise Indra and Agni—another further stage of advanced guard—for being the fount of poetry. This implies that creators, sages, poets and mortals were bound together in a seamless and flexible reality in which the *created* could not only break into the ranks of their *creators* but were in a constant process of actively producing a part of the seamless reality at their own level. Thus, various levels of advanced guard, with their respective levels and registers of discourse, and various ways of articulating reality, followed and learnt from the people who occupied the level above them. However, these stages were not stratified and the occupants of one level could actually move to the next if they could master the discourse and register of that level. Sharma (1996) also points out that *stotra* and *kavya*, for instance, were two ways of discoursing that were often used interchangeably for one another. He (1996, p. 18) goes on to remark: "The *kavi* (poet) can be knowledgeable. There's no opposition between knowledge and poetry." What this, in effect, means is that in pre-feudal Vedic times there was no opposition between various registers and forms of discourse and the creative and the critical complemented one another and often commingled. There was neither any hierarchisation nor any competition among them.

According to Sharma (1996), the whole of Rig Veda and parts of the later Vedas, show how various forms or registers of discourse existed together in complementary harmony. But all that changed when the Aryanised pastoral-nomadic and primitive agrarian socio-economic formations moved towards feudalism. The stratification of the various levels of the advanced guard and the freezing of the social order into a rigid hierarchy that accompanied the ascendancy of feudalism, has been revealed rather accurately in Sankrityayan's (1942) fictionalised account of a historical (Upanishadic) period with the mythical king Pravahan as its protagonist. The short story shows how, with the advent of feudalism in a large part of the subcontinent circa 700 BC, the Brahmins (priests) and Kshatriyas (rulers) were formed as two different rigid strata from the same family of clan (or tribe) superiors in order to ensure a smooth sharing of landed property without any feud.

Sharma (1996) maps these changes in the realm of intellectual production and brings to light the fact that the Vedas that came after the first Rig Veda kept tilting towards *karmakanda* (ritualism). Consequently, *purohit*, which was another designation for *kavi* (poet), came to be a synonym for a Brahmin priest only. With the coming of the Upanishads, Sharma tells us, we can already see a hierarchical stratification, both in the realm of discourses and that of their contemporary social formation. Increased stratification that accompanied the consolidation of feudalism in this part of the world led to each strata or caste having its own corresponding discourse of making reality. And the linguistic-philosophical-literary notions or Sanskrit, Prakrit, Lokayat, etc., emphasise the rigidly pyramidal structure of feudalism in the realm of ideas as also in the larger social formation.

The ideology of the contemplative individual and modern form of art that emerged during the Renaissance gradually freed discourses in their multiple forms and registers from the stratified hierarchy of feudalism. But there was a price to be paid. The bourgeois ethic of individuated production and passive consumption, so integral to modern art, not only created a split between the producer and the consumer, it also led to a rift within different genres. Instead of their earlier complementarity, artistic and literary forms and registers congealed into genres, which competed with each other and became oppositional. This *laissez-faire* of forms and genres, by virtue of the monopolistic intent that is at the heart of the free market logic, only served to *otherise* one genre from the next. Benjamin (1984, p. 224) writes: "'Opposites that in happier periods fertilized one another have become insoluble antinomies. Thus science and belles-letteres, criticism and production, education and politics, fall apart in disorder...'." The system of aesthetics that has consequently evolved, is not only premised on this bourgeois opposition of artistic forms, but also serves to strengthen it and its commodity character by often privileging its own (criticalist) forms over what it calls intuitive, creative or sensory ways of apprehending reality. The most appropriate instance would, perhaps, be Hegel's theory of aesthetics. Hegel scholar Michael Inwood (1993, p. xxiv), in his introduction to Hegel's *Introductory Lectures on Aesthetics,* summarises the philosopher's view on art: "Art reveals the absolute, and so, in their different ways, do religion and philosophy. Art thus expresses the same 'content' as religion and philosophy, but in a different 'form'. It expresses its content in a sensory form, while religion does so in the form of pictorial imagery (*Vorstellung*) and philosophy in the form of conceptual thought. Philosophy is higher than art, both because conceptual thought is the essence of man and because conceptual thought is the essence of man and because philosophy has a wider range. Philosophy can speak about art, but art cannot speak in any detail about philosophy...."

Any Marxist praxis of art will have to transcend this realm of the oppositional. For, only by attempting to do so can it address the bourgeois problem of alienated production and consumption. Althusser (1971, p. 223), whose sole mission in life was to ferret out every last trace of bourgeois-Hegelian thought from Marxism, unfortunately fell prey to this reification (or commodity fetishism) of opposition of forms when he entered the domain of art and aesthetics: "The difference between art and science lies in the *specific form* in which they give us the same object in quite different ways: art in the form of 'seeing' and 'perceiving' or 'feeling', science in the form of *knowledge* (in the strict sense, by concepts)." (Emphases author's.) Althusser's astute *scientific* discourse of Marxism had failed to escape ideological contamination on this count.

The instance above should serve to make Marxists more cautious in their efforts to *theorise* on art. Benjamin (1984, p. 228), perhaps, provides us with the most nuanced Marxist understanding between art practices and aesthetics (theory). He quotes Brecht to assert that the "functional transformation" of the apparatus of production "in accordance with socialism...to the utmost extent possible" is the only way in which this battle against individuated production and passive consumption can be fought in the world of ideas, discourses and creativity. Only a step in the direction of creating a socialist mode of universal production—where every act of consumption is an immediate and simultaneous gesture of production—can de-ideologise and de-commodify art, making it a zone of critique and class struggle.

Marxist Praxis of Art: A Random Survey

Individuated production, which is the ethos of art in its current forms, is embedded in the matrix of contemplative individuality. This idea, as we have seen earlier, embodied a progressive impulse since it enabled human beings to question and battle feudal hierarchy and oppression. And the new notions of sociality that resulted from this idea and its related ethic of production were, therefore, obviously liberating and emancipatory. However, the ethic of individuated production is bound inextricably, in a dialectical dynamic, with the capitalist mode of production. Therefore, things or ideas produced in this process can be accessed only through dissemination channels specific to this mode of production. The free market is the congealment of those channels. The modern art product, with the ethic of individuated production at its core was, therefore, naturally produced for the market through which its *consumers* could access it. Art, which is so in the modern sense precisely because it is a commodity to be consumed, was a liberating phenomenon in the era of capitalism's rise pitted against a declining feudalism. But capital and its marketplace have their own laws of perpetuation, expansion and intensification. The generation of surplus value and protracted accumulation of capital ensure the survival of capitalism and its market. The logic of capital accumulation through extraction of surplus value also makes sure that there is an intensification of market processes so that capitalism can flourish and thrive. There are many interrelated processes of "value transfer" by which capitalism generates surplus value. We shall, for now, deal with only one part: the fluctuation of prices. The structural logic of the market, where everybody is free to buy and sell his/her products and thus compete against one another, brings about a fixing of prices for various commodities. This means that every product, irrespective of its use-value, has an exchange-value, which is created the moment it enters the market and is commodified. This exchange-value, an abstraction, can be seen in its reified concreteness in the price of a commodity and the money that changes hands during transaction. The structural logic of the market varies this exchange-value, in accordance with the laws of demand and supply, to keep the process of surplus-value generation going.

Modern art, since it had simultaneously created the art mart for its accessing, had to, as part of the process of production and consumption it had unleashed, subordinate its use-value to its exchange-value. This was the only way its market and, therefore, its productive logic could survive and grow. As a result, the use-value of art at its inception during the Renaissance—of critiquing feudalism's oppressive stratifications and in the process creating *just, liberal* and *humane* ideas of a deinstrumentalised social order that was constitutive of autonomy—was finally taken over by consumption for its own sake, that is the rule of exchange-value. Modern art, by conceiving itself as such, had sealed its fate, its initial progressive impulses notwithstanding. Marx (1954, p. 46) writes: "...exchange-value is the only form in which the value of commodities can manifest itself or be expressed."

Adorno (1991) tells us that the process of consumption for its own sake is reified by the structural logic of commodity capitalism to create ideologies like the utilitarian entertainment industry and the realm of "pure" and "useless" high art. In this realm, contemplative individualism is a faint shadow of its original progressive self as the individual selves of authors, artists, musicians or actors are mere appendages of their commodities. Their individualities are crucial, but only insofar as they serve to advertise these commodities of theirs—that is, enabling their selling and justifying their prices or exchange-values. The star-artist and his valorised individuality is nothing more than a commodity fetish. In such a scenario, works of pre-capitalist creativity, which were produced in collectivities like guilds and *gharanas* and which do not bear the imprint of individual uniqueness, are relegated to the margins of the art world as repetitive (Vasari) and 'inferior' forms, and are consumed as craft for their exoticised 'primitivity'. An active Marxist critique of this ideology of art will, therefore, have to locate works of art or artistic practices that problematise this cult of the individual in the realm of modern aesthetics. Marx (1976, p. 617) states in his ninth thesis on Feurbach: "The highest point reached by contemplative materialism, that is, materialism which does not comprehend sensuousness as practical activity, is the contemplation of single individuals and of civil society." Some modern avant-garde works of art and artistic practices have problematised the unlocated and 'universal' individual, who is an a priori source of reality without he himself being a part of it and, therefore, not yielding to his own objective investigation.

The ideology of (bourgeois) realism—which informed all of post-Renaissance literature and art and which continues to be the organising principle for much of recent artistic and literary productions as well—has at its centre the individual author. His voice or perspective narrativising and ordering reality. Within such realist works of art there is only one narrative of reality possible and the individual narrator's narrating voice cannot in turn become its own object. This is much like in our lives, where reality, according to the ruling elite and the dominant classes, is the universal reality for all; even those who do not belong to that class but have a false consciousness of their interests being identical to that of the ruling class.

Even Soviet-style socialist realism—its influence visible, even now, on a large swathe of Indian regional writing, particularly Hindi—which valorises the proletarian hero, the rebel or the sceptical outsider grappling with his Sisyphean reality, is imbued with this spirit of bourgeois realism. The former's break with the latter is only normative. In such works of literature, the narrative voice is unquestioned and it never becomes its own object, that is, the narrative itself. This has been true of 'progressive' Sartrean existentialism and much of 'engaged' literature that has followed it.

Barthes (1968), however, has provided readers with an alternative canon of, what he termed, "zero-degree writing". In such writing the work is its own narrative object. The language of the narrative subject folds upon itself. Such literature does not represent a reality outside itself, but describes its own self. The writing—or the narrative, or the authorial voice—becomes its own object. The French New Novel movement, which began in the 1950s, with Alain Robbe-Grillet (1965) in the lead, is one of the prime exemplars of such writing. Foucault (19887, p. 9) summed up the aesthetic of another "zero-degree" writer, Maurice Blanchot, rather succinctly in the assertion 'I speak'. Foucault (1987, p. 10) writes:

> "...the two propositions hidden in the statement ('I speak' and 'I say I speak') in no way compromise each other. I am protected by the impenetrable fortress of the assertion's self-assertion, by the way it coincides exactly with itself, leaving no jagged edges, averting all danger of error by saying no more than that I am speaking. Neither in the words in question nor in the subject that pronounces them is there an obstacle or insinuation to come between the object-proposition and the proposition that states it. It is therefore true, undeniably true, that I am speaking when I say that I am speaking."

"Zero degree writing" problematised the realist novel and its modern successors by negating the ideology of an external reality that is represented in the individual author's perspective and in his narrative voice, by making the subject the object of its own literary or artistic inquiry. This not only effected a complete shift in the techniques of narrativisation, but also transformed the understanding about language and its use. The language of conventional realism is the language of the unproblematised narrator-individual. And since the problem of the unlocated individual is the ideology of bourgeois modes of being, the narrator-individual of conventional realism holds all the virtues and vices of a bourgeois selfhood.

In the era of advanced capitalism, the language that we have is naturally the metalanguage of bourgeois being. All word, phrases and syntaxes of all kinds of languages—spoken, written, visual, auditory, and so on—besides signifying the reality that was held in them before their mythologisation also produce meanings of other reified realities of bourgeois ideological origin (Barthes, 1993). Barthes provides us with an instance of such mythologisation when he holds before us the picture of a Black man saluting the French flag that had appeared in a popular French magazine. The photograph, besides denoting the obviously apparent reality of an individual saluting a flag, also connotes the fact that Blacks are full citizens of the White French nation. Thus the relationship between denotation and connotation is relational. Only when an ideologised meaning is produced by the reification of a new social relation of production that accompanies the intensification of capitalism and worms its way into a language and is *connoted* by it, the reality that this language signified before the production of this new meaning becomes *denotative.*

Robbe-Grillet's novels and poems of Francis Ponge (1998) attempt to shatter the bourgeois self by producing works that get posited as metaphors seeking to critique and destroy its metalanguage by pushing it to its neutral denotative state. Language and words in their writings seek to denote themselves and they do not form a metalingual universe of bourgeois myths where these words and language, in fulfilling their denotative function, have to move beyond that and connote an ideological representational reality. Most of Ponge's poems (like 'Rain', 'Ripe Blackberries', 'The Crate', 'The Cigarette', The Orange' and so on) deal with things only as they *neutrally* and *objectively* appear and not for what more they could mean or represent.

In a different setting, Hindi poet Vinod Kumar Shukla (1996) has attempted similar effects in his poetry. An example:

> *Subah chhay baje ka waqt, subah chhay baje ki tarah.*
> *Ped ke niche aadmi tha,*
> *Kuhre mein aadmi ke dhabbe ke andar wah aadmi tha.*
> *Ped ka dhabba bilkul ped ki tarah tha.*
> *Dahiney raddi nasl ke ghode ka dhabba,*
> *Raddi nasl ke Ghode ki tarah tha.*
> *...Aur kai makan, kai ped, kai*
> *Sadken ityadi koi ghoda nahin tha.*

(The time six in the morning was like six in the morning./ There was a man under the tree,/ Inside the silhouette of a man in the fog he was that man./ The stain of the tree was exactly like the tree./ On the right, the stain of the horse from a rotten breed,/ Was like the horse from that rotten breed./...And many houses, many trees, many/streets etcetera, none of them was the horse.) (Translation mine.)

The only accusation one can level against such examples of zero degree writing is that they lapse into solipsism and thus, by extension, into subjective idealism. But such charges are easily laid to rest when one sees that they operate within modes of bourgeois artistic representation, dialectically refracting one another.

But it is not zero degree writing alone that problematises conventional realism. Turkish writer Orhan Pamuk's (2001) *My Name is Red,* set in 16th century Turkey when the European Renaissance is on its ascendancy even as the Islamic world was slowly but surely falling into decline, is an excellent example of such problematisation. Without taking any recourse to zero degree writing, and spinning a cracking period yarn, Pamuk attempts to critique the humanising Renaissance by pitting the aperspectival aesthetic of Islamic miniatures against the perspectivism of Renaissance art. He very cleverly shows how miniatures without any sense of perspective open up a multiplicity of perspectives on reality, whereas perspectivism of Renaissance art fixes reality and establishes the authority of only one way of ordering it. That of the artist or the writer. Pamuk's critique, however, is not limited to the content of the novel, it is reflected by its form as well. The narrative of *My Name...* proceeds, not through the authorial voice of a single subject, but is constituted by a mélange of stories being told by different characters. Pamuk's novel, therefore, fractures the singular authorial discourse into a Babel of multiple perspectives, just the quality he attributes to Islamic miniatures. However, we should realise that this multiplicity of discourses and perspectives is something that did not originally exist in the pre-Renaissance and aperspectival Islamic world. Pamuk, situated as he is within the post-Renaissance paradigm, consciously (mis)reads multiperspectivism into aperspectival miniatures. He reorders a historical reality, post facto, with the help of his present-day rationality, to problematise it. Consequently, the aperspectival multiplicity of *kissa goi* refracts the narrative mode of the novel and fractures it. On the other hand, the present-day rationality of the novelistic discourse is the space within which these multiple discourses and perspectives are situated. That is the dialectic of such art.

Both zero degree writing and the works of writers like Pamuk present us with a classic case of neurosis. The language (or metalanguage) that we possess is either used to access realities that are outside it, or are pushed to its limits so that it can represent only its denotative realities. This neurotic hovering of the language, and the self from which it emanates, near their death is what constitutes for Barthes (1975) the "pleasure of the text". And aren't pleasure and desire necessary ingredients of revolutionary political action? Foucault (1983, p. xii) acknowledges their relationship when he asks: "How can and must desire deploy its forces within the political domain and grow more intense in the process of overturning the established order?"

However, in both these instances, is it not finally the novel with the author's name embossed on its cover—emphasising the ethic of individuated production and alienated consumption—that appropriates and makes the representation of such subversive discourses possible? The answer is in the affirmative and that is exactly why Marxists should intervene as active readers, wrenching the subversions from the domain of unproblematised and thus commodified discourse of the novel as a product in the publishing market and an ideology reinforcing bourgeois civil society, and restore their revolutionary sting to them by making apparent the kind of political-economic rationality they originate from.

Jorge Luis Borges (1993) is a supreme example of such an active reader. In inventing zero degree writing in his own inimitable style by making literature its own subject, Borges refused to merely consume literature but joined in its simultaneous production. For instance, his modern fables, centering on imaginary books and libraries, myths, legends, and stories, grew visibly out of literature that he read. 'Pierre Menard, Author of Don Quixote', 'The Library of Babel' and

'Tlon, Uqbar, Orbius Tertius', are some instances that elucidate his literary practice and discourse.

Similar active readers, who refuse to passively consume the reality presented to them but want to participate in its making and transformation, are envisaged and realised in Brecht's epic theatre. The epic theatre audiences are meant to no longer identify with a 'familiar' reality on stage, but are estranged from this familiarity (alienated from an alien familiarity, negation of negation) so they reflect on it and analyse the processes that constitute it. Brecht (2001, p. 5) writes: "The spectator was no longer in any way allowed to submit to an experience uncritically (and without practical consequences) by means of simple empathy with the characters in a play. The production took the subject-matter and the incidents shown and put them through a process of alienation: the alienation that is necessary to all understanding." In practice, Brecht realised this by introducing commentary (newspaper clippings, bits of radio news, newsreels, etc.) in the middle of a play to explain its unfolding. Brecht's productions thus become artistic spaces where the opposition between the 'experiential' and the 'critical' is obliterated.

Boal (2000, p. 155), in his "theatre of the oppressed", takes the Brechtian aesthetic to its logical culmination. In his productions, not only does the audience reflect critically on the reality being depicted on the stage, it begins participating in and determining the unfolding of the play. In the process, the performer/spectator dichotomy is abolished and so is the producer/consumer split. "*The poetics of the oppressed* is essentially the poetics of liberation: the spectator no longer delegates power to the characters either to think or to act in his place. The spectator frees himself; he thinks and acts for himself! Theater is action!" (Emphasis author's.)

Conclusion

Such active reading or making of reality transforms art. It is no longer an ideology to be passively consumed, but a technology to change and produce reality, facilitating universal and complete control over the production process.

Only when this Marxist praxis of art is in place, will the Fascist tableaux of discipline, power and violence cease to inspire people from an alienated distance. Only then will we have transformed art into class struggle.

REFERENCES

Adorno, Theodor W., *The Culture Industry* (Routledge, London, 1991)

Althusser, Louis, 'Ideology and Ideological State Apparatuses'. *In Lenin and Philosophy and Other Essays* (Monthly Review Press, New York, 1971)

Althusser, Louis, A Letter on Art'. In *Lenin and Philosophy and Other Essays* (Monthly Review Press, New York, 1971)

Bakhtin, Mikhail M., *The Dialogic Imagination,* ed. Michael Holquist, tr. Caryl Emerson and Michael Holquist (University of Texas Press, Austin, 1981)

Barthes, Roland, *Writing Degree Zero,* tr. Annette Lavers and Colin Smith (Hill and Wang, New York, 1968)

Barthes, Roland, *Mythologies,* tr. Annette Lavers (Vintage, London, 1993)

Barthes, Roland, *The Pleasure of the Text,* tr. Richard Miller (Hill and Wang, New York, 1975)

Benjamin, Walter, 'The Work of Art in the Age of Mechanical Reproduction'. In *Illuminations,* tr. Harry Zohn (Fontana Press, London, 1992)

Benjamin, Walter, 'The Author as Producer'. In *Reflections,* tr. Edmund Jephcott (Schocken Books, New York, 1986)

Boal, Augusto, *Theater of the Oppressed,* tr. Charles A. and Maria-Odilia Leel McBride and Emily Fryer (Pluto Press, London, 2000)

Borges, Jorge Luis, *Ficciones,* tr. Anthony Kerrigan, Alastair Reed, Anthony Bonner, Helen Temple and Ruthven Todd (Everyman's Library, London, 1993)

Brecht, Bertolt, 'Brecht on Theatre'. In *Modern European Drama—Background Prose Readings* (Worldview Publications, New Delhi, 2001)

Burckhardt, Jacob, *The Civilization of the Renaissance in Italy* (Modern Library, New York, 1995)

Foucault, Michel, 'Maurice Blanchot: The Thought From Outside'. In *Foucault/Blanchot*, tr. Brain Massumi and Jeffrey Mehlman (Zone Books, New York, 1990)

Foucault, Michel, 'Preface'. In Gilles Deleuze and Felix Guattari, *Anti-Oedipus*, tr. Robert Hurley, Mark Seem and Helen R. Lane (The Athlone Press, London, 1983)

Inwood, Michael, 'Introduction'. In G.W.F. Hegel, *Introductory Lectures on Aesthetics*, tr. Bernard Bosanquet (Penguin, London, 1993)

Levi-Strauss, Claude, *The Savage Mind* (The University of Chicago Press, 1966)

Marx, Karl, *Capital* (Volume I), tr. Samuel Moore and Edward Aveling (Progress Publishers, Moscow, 1976)

Marx, Karl, 'Theses on Feurbach'. In Karl Marx and Frederick Engels, *The German Ideology* (Progress Publishers, Moscow, 1976)

Ponge, Francis, *Selected Poems*, tr. Margaret Guiton, Johan Montague and C.K. Williams (Faber and Faber, London, 1998)

Panofsky, Erwin, *Perspective as Symbolic Form* (Zone Books, New York, 1991)

Pamuk, Orhan, *My Name is Red*, tr. Erdag M. Goknar (Faber and Faber, London, 2001)

Ray, Sibnarayan, 'Renaissance o Itihashtatva'. In *Prabandha Sangraha* 2 (Ananda, Calcutta, 2002)

Robbe-Grillet, Alain, *Two Novels By Robbe-Grillet* (*Jealousy* and *In the Labyrinth*), tr. Richard Howard (Grove Press, New York, 1965)

Sankrityayan, Rahul, 'Pravahan'. In *Volga se Ganga* (Kitab Mahal, Allahabad, 1942)

Sharma, Ramvilas, *Bharatiya Sahitya ki Bhumika* (Rajkamal Prakashan, New Delhi, 1996)

Shukla, Vinod Kumar, *Woh Aadmi Naya Garam Coat Pahinkar Chala Gaya Vichar Ki Tarah* (Aadhar Prakashan, Panchkula, Haryana, 1996)

Vasari, Giorgio, *Lives of Artists* (Volume I and II), tr. George Bull) (Penguin, London, 1987).

3

Academics, Politics and Class Struggle

"The Owl of Minerva flies only at dusk" is a Hegelian maxim that permeates our reflection on the everydayness of our modern living. Thinking for all of us here, thanks to this maxim, is now a process that is self-conscious—some would say painfully so—of its retrospective fate vis-à-vis an event. Clearly, the process of thinking seeks to make sense of, explicate and give a discursive rationality to an event after it has *happened*. Thought and reason can then be said to be traces left behind by an event that has *occurred* and in *occurring* has disappeared. What we, given our specific conjuncture, ought to do now is complete this Hegelian awareness by comprehending the fact that the "dusk" of post-facto cognition is a movement, yet again, towards the dawn of the event and its non-rational return. The flapping of the Owl of Minerva's wings in flight should, in fact, be envisaged not merely as the thought on an event that has occurred thereby anticipating its return, but as the re-enactment of the event—which occurred in the moment of so-called political action—and its singular, synthetic, critical processuality in the moment or condition of human thought itself.

In the cognitively anticipated return of the event the event actually returns, of course, in that moment of thinking, even as it presages yet again its own non-rational return in another moment of political action or pragmatics. Hegel's Owl of Minerva, through this self-reflexive optic, can morph into the revolutionary subjectivity of Marx's proletariat. And *'academics beyond academia' is the conceptual common name that we could give to this emergence of revolutionary subjectivity in the moment of human thinking or knowledge.*

It is this term that would, for us, *serve to programmatically encapsulate the task of working-class politics on the terrain of institutionalised academics and the university it is constitutive of.* But before we get ahead of ourselves, we must recognise why this task of academic revolutionary politics impinges on our consciousness with such pressing urgency. So much so that we have gathered here today, one must add belatedly, to thrash out the issues on that particular count.

The Political Terrain of Academics

Whether or not we on the Left agree with the specific programmatic unity of strategy and tactics posed by the Maoist movement in and from its agrarian-tribal location, it would certainly be disingenuous on our part not to accept the fact that the ongoing Maoist insurgency has posed the larger question of working-class revolution not merely as a passive object of a clinically discursive inquiry, but first and foremost as an agenda of active political action and expression. That said, we must also acknowledge that this insurgency—which is little more than a series of sensational strikes persistently launched by the Maoist PLGA and people's militias in their areas of dominance—is symptomatic of the retreat the working-class revolution as a whole is in today.

Nevertheless, *the unavoidable need to stage that revolution on the ground of the university and canonised academics is something that ought to unite both the upholders and left-wing critics of the Indian Maoist movement.* That the former should see this as an unfolding of the revolutionary logic posited by the Maoist people's war, even as the latter see in this an opportunity to rectify the distortion of the revolutionary project by the "Narodnik populism" of the Maoists does not detract from the given task and thus their unity on that count.

The task of envisaging the university and the institutionalised knowledge-production that is constitutive of it into a terrain of class struggle can be broadly divided into three formally specific but logically united levels or moments.

The first and the most immediately obvious and accessible is the moment of the struggle by students, teachers and other staff members *to control the university*—much like the history of workers' struggles to control factories internationally—to run it in terms of both autonomous determination of curriculum and pedagogy, and administration of the larger social life on campus through a process of active and vigorous participatory democracy.

The second level is, of course, the moment of struggle *to reconstitute the hierarchical pedagogical relation* between the teacher and the taught into a completely horizontal space. A space where, following the lessons of critical pedagogue Paulo Freire, the educator himself has to be educated and where the univocal and monologic pedagogical relation is envisaged merely as a provisional one with which the reconstituted teaching process begins, only to be eventually abolished in the course of that process.

Last but not least, it is about *transforming the grammar or logic of academic production of canonised knowledge and the subjectivity such knowledge-production concomitantly engenders.* This transformation would be of a philosophised, a priori, transhistorical subjectivity—which is constitutive of a representative modality of knowledge creation that is contingent on the alienating and hierarchical rift between the subject and the object—into an autonomous expression of the concrete where subjectivity is nothing but the organic expression of the singular, synthetic, processual concrete. This expression of the singular, processual concrete is articulated only in and through a relationship of critique, vis-a-vis the reigning subjectivity of the dualised realm of pedagogic determination. It is this critically oppositional subjectivity of the singular that embodies a critique of political economy, wherein the differential circulation of value and thus differential distribution of power, and their constitutive productive logic of value creation, is sought to be decimated through active, politically materialised critique, which is another name for revolution. There is absolutely no doubt that the three levels just described are discrete only in a conceptual sense and are, in the actual operation of materialised politics, not only simultaneously accessible but continually, if not continuously, spill over into each other. It is in that context that we would do well, as of now, to tactically privilege the third moment over the first two in terms of envisaging a programme of revolutionary working-class politics on the terrain of the university.

That the vigorously participatory democratic control of the university by students, teachers and other staff members is not essentially an administrative question, insofar as administration is the bourgeois mode of politics (or anti-politics), must be grasped by the collectivity of the movement that seeks to take such control. That collectivity ought to subjectively realise that for its movement the question of administration of the university is an epiphenomenon, an afterimage in Benjamin's words, of the critical-oppositional impulse of the politics of autonomy. *For, such democratic control, precisely in seeking to render pedagogical relations and techniques, curriculum, and the total modality of social life in and around the university autonomous by seeking to free them from the administrative determination of work, which is alienation of labour from its autonomous, creative and contingent human essence, expresses the tendency to abolish the totality of the process called capital accumulation.* This process is embodied in the form of work, which splits human livelihood into alienated domains of production (work) and reproduction (leisure and work for leisure). The culture of administrative determination that completely permeates both these domains is intrinsic to and expression of the alienating logic of work. The *university is, to that extent, an emblematic site of capitalism as it is one of those few domains of capital where the determination of alienating work is apparent both in the register of reproduction (for students-becoming-workers) and production (teachers, researchers, other staff members but also students).* It is, therefore, one of those rare sites where labour can be seen in more than one of its alterities, sometimes in the same moment, and where Marx's conceptualisation of the collective worker to indicate the always formational character of the working class becomes almost empirically discernible and *actual*.

Clearly then, a movement that seeks to take control of the university, if envisaged without any subjective realisation of its constitutive logic of positing a critique of political economy in its totality, is bound to reify its afterimage of administration and, consequently, be subsumed yet again into the very social configuration of capitalist class power it had sought to challenge and supersede. *The subjectivity of the movement should be such that it envisages the movement as one that seeks to free the question of human livelihood from the grip of work and capital accumulation through a critical opposition to the bourgeois form of what is called the real economy, even as it in the same movement seeks to transform the pursuit of academics for students, researchers and teachers alike into a continuous expression of critique of the externally imposed discipline and drudgery of work it now is*. Such a critique, needless to say, would simultaneously be constitutive of the unalienated human creativity that its operation as critique seeks in the first place.

The latter is nothing but the enactment of the total critique of political economy of capital at one local moment, even as through that enactment it indicates and moves towards re-enacting that essential critique yet again in another local moment manifest as the so-called real economy.

Academics beyond Academia or "Class Struggle in the Theoretical Moment?

Our tactical privileging of the third moment of *the struggle to transform the philosophised structure, and thus the hierarchised, invasive and instrumentalised grammar, of academic knowledge-production would enable the collectivity of the movement for participatory democratic control of the university to grasp and simultaneously subjectivise the essential link between the moment of the university and the form of the bourgeois 'real' economy as such*. That is because constitutive of this process of transforming the instrumentalised and hierarchised grammar of academically canonised knowledge production is a critical and autonomous subjectivity. Something that embodies not only the manoeuvre of class struggle in the moment of theory but through the self-reflexive expression of its formation and emergence as an enactment of critical singularity at that moment becomes an allegory of negativity with regard to the moment of work in both the university and bourgeois 'real' economy. The critical and autonomous subjectivity constitutive of this struggle or process of transforming the philosophised structure and instrumentalised grammar of academic knowledge-production, due to the self-reflexivity of that subjectivity, is thus, very clearly, also an allegory for the unfolding of the unalienated processual logic through its determinate re-enactment at other moments of capitalist contradiction through a critique of and opposition to the alienated, dualised and antagonistic concrete situations at each of those moments. Needless to say that such self-reflexivity, which the form of the transformative struggle at the theoretical moment expresses, implies the negation of its form as such for other moments so that this form's foundational and constitutive logic of infinite processuality can be generalised and then reclaimed in its multiple formal specificities at other different historical-ontological moments.

It is this double movement of the theoretical struggle, staged at the location of institutionalised academics, that renders its manifest form into revolutionary theory a la Lenin. We have chosen to call it *academics beyond academia*. But the perfectly legitimate question that arises here is why do we still choose to stick to the term academics, given that it is thoroughly implicated in a transhistorical, hypostatised and philosophised subjectivity, even as we seek to transgress the subject/object dichotomy constitutive of such subjectivity. We could as well ask, why doesn't the formulation *"class struggle in the theoretical moment"* suffice.

That is because the form in which the struggle manifests itself at the theoretical moment is important insofar as it has a bearing on other moments, like that of pragmatics say, by way of allegorically alluding through its self-reflexivity to the logic of unalienated processuality, which its determinate affirmation of autonomy enacts through a critical negation of the subjectivated centre of the realm of alienation, duality, representation and antagonism. Clearly, the form through which the logic of unalienated and infinite processuality is critically enacted at the moment of theory needs to be conceptualised not so as to effect the pedagogical and externalised imposition of the concept on another moment but because that concept could allegorically remind us of the universal logic of unalienated processuality it enacted by way of critically asserting its autonomy in relation to the reigning subjectivity of alienation, duality and representation in the determinate condition of theory. That reminder to reclaim or re-enact the logic of unalienated, processual concrete is necessary as without that *memory* the opposition to the reigning subjectivated centres of alienation, duality and contradiction at other moments would remain caught in the constitutive antithetical fetish of duality and competition, and would fail to become critical. That would also mean the unfolding of the processual revolutionary logic, which emerged through the form of class struggle in the theoretical moment, has been stymied. *Therefore, the concept of academics beyond academia is not a concept in the pedagogical sense but in the allegorical sense, whereby it is not a concept only by virtue of being one that is self-reflexively indicative of its own subsequent formal negation. So, the knowledge of unalienated singular processual logic of universality, which is encapsulated in 'academics beyond academia', the conceptualised form of class struggle at the moment of canonised academics, can only be remembered as that concept so that it can be repeatedly extracted and enacted anew at every other lived concrete moment of capitalist duality and contradiction.*

It is this dialectical awareness of the concept about itself that is fatally absent from the formulation *class struggle in the theoretical moment*. For, even as that concept arises, not very differently from 'academics beyond academia', through the enactment and affirmation of the logic of autonomous and unalienated processuality in the process of critically negating the subjectivated centre of the total system of alienation, duality, hierarchy, representation, and invasive objectification of knowledge, it *tends to reify the form through which the critical subjectivity of the processual had determinately appeared in the specific moment of theory.* As a result, its relation with other historically different moments of capitalist duality and contradiction becomes pedagogical, thereby undermining the entire logic of reclaiming and re-enacting the working-class subjectivity of the singular-universal in a determinate manner.

Theodor Adorno's formulation that his "was the theoretical moment of class struggle", which informed not merely his own politico-theoretical practice and position but that of the entire post-war Frankfurt School, clearly illustrates a problem that one wishes to term his and his School's Heideggerian tangle. This problem deserves our special attention because it plagues many of our comrades in the academia, who profess to one strain or school of leftwing radical politics or another. *They clearly content themselves by restricting their politics of critique to the theoretical moment,* even as they refuse to accept the fact that the form in which their critical politics has emerged in the academic moment of theory self-reflexively cries out to be unfolded through re-enactment of the constitutive processual logic of that theoretical form of critical politics into the messy moment of political pragmatics or, what some of them label with barely suppressed derision as, "mobilisational politics". They usually meet the demands that the moment of political pragmatics, which for them is a realm of irredeemably uncritical and positivist abstraction, with disengaged pessimism and that classically Adornesque melancholy. This melancholic quietism of theirs with regard to the moment of pragmatics and political action is nothing but the manifestation of their failed attempt to pedagogically impose the form in which their critical politics emerged in the moment of academic theory. *An attempt that would fail—even if it were not to be repelled by the dogmatic pedagogues of party politics and pragmatism—by undermining the entire revolutionary project of continuously unfolding the subjectivity of singular processuality by re-enacting it in a determinate fashion at various other concrete moments of capitalist contradiction.*

As a matter of fact, this Heideggerian problem of our Adornoesquely academic Marxists, who have come to constitute a silent but rather resilient hegemony in the realm of so-called radical political theory at the academic moment, at least since the Soviet debacle, has turned out to be no less noxious than the problem of our dogmatic party bosses and their sundry organisational apparatchiks. The latter have reified and sought to pedagogically impose the form through which the revolutionary subjectivity of unalienated processuality expressed itself at either the Fordist industrial worker's location or the agrarian-tribal location in the moment of pragmatics on other locations within the moment of pragmatics or, more dangerously, on the moment of theory and knowledge, thereby denying it its determinate specificity.

"Doing Philosophy under the Condition of Politics"

The working-class struggle is, not surprisingly, caught today between the rock of chronic quietism, as far as the relation as it unfolds from the moment of theory to the moment of pragmatics goes; and the hard-place of dogmatism, as far as the unfolding of the essential relation from the moment of pragmatics to that of theory is concerned. The result, for the project of reconstituting a revolutionary theory, has, as a consequence, been dismal. *Theory, in the specificity of its moment of theoretical practice, has become a deconstructionist game of constantly proliferating pluralities, which certainly talks of power but means nothing as it refuses to ground that power in the relations among its various configurations of materiality.* On the other hand, pragmatics, in the specificity of its moment of various practices and thus also positing the theories of those various practices, has fallen prey to the tyranny of pragmatism, which has repressed all possibility of constructing a revolutionary theory.

The contradiction between the two positions—of quietist deconstructionism in the theoretical moment and dogmatically positivist pragmatism in the moment of pragmatics—is, as we can see, merely apparent. In reality, they are embedded in the same structure of transhistorical and instrumentalised subjectivity of canonised (bourgeois) philosophy. Our conceptualisation of 'academics beyond academia' is an attempt to conceptualise the manoeuvre of dialectically negating and superseding this contradiction. And on this score, one could argue, that *this project of academics beyond academia has a stronger kinship with Louis Althusser (and Alain Badiou's) classically Leninist concept of "doing philosophy under the condition of politics", than the one-sided formulation of Adorno of "this" being "the theoretical moment of class struggle".* True, Althusser, in his later writings, did dub philosophy as a state-form. But the question he repeatedly broached through the totality of his politico-theoretical practice, and which remains even today the most important politico-theoretical question for working-class politics, is, can there be a philosophy in the negative? Something that becomes, for the theoretical moment, the Leninist transition-state-form? That is, can philosophy be a modality to affirm the unalienated, singular processuality implicit in the critical negation of the subjectivated centre of the horizon of alienation, duality, hierarchy and contradiction?

In other words, can the logic of unalienated processuality be located in a form, idiom, ontology or subjectivity, which has emerged to express its autonomy through critique of the realm of alienation, hierarchy and representation? Can there be a philosophically affirmative explication and description of what such a form or subjectivity says in terms of why and how it says what it says and not merely in terms of what it apparently says as a form or subjectivity per se? It is the constant posing of these questions that our project of academics beyond academia is tasked with. This, and nothing else, is the task of revolution today.

In that context, we would do well to delineate the exact difference between Adorno's critical theoretical idea of class struggle in the theoretical moment with Althusser's apparently similar project of envisaging the academic discipline of philosophy as a terrain of politics and class struggle. And this one intends to do through a rather schematic comparison between the politico-theoretical practices and stances of these two luminaries of Western Marxism, if only to show that Althusser's practice, notwithstanding its 'theoreticist' misinterpretation by both his followers and detractors, enables us to stake out a much more militant working-class position than Adorno's infamous theoretical melancholy would ever allow. Of course, this exercise is not supported by an exegetical mining of their respective texts, something that is par for the course in rigorous academic debates but something from which an interloper is exempt, considering that most 'academic' Marxists expect no more than the 'dilettantish' and schematic forays into the realm of theory by their brethren from the world of pragmatics. One has every intention to live up to that reputation and no intention to prove otherwise. So, without any further ado one would wish to rush like a fool in the direction of one's schema, even as one beckons, fruitlessly perhaps, at one's angelic academic friends to follow suit.

Let us begin with the negative example of Adorno first. The philosopher's essay on Brecht, to cite Brazilian cultural theorist Roberto Schwarz, "knows and criticizes Brecht's political-aesthetic positions, places greater emphasis on the work than on the theory; or rather it sees the role of the latter inside the former". Clearly, Adorno in his reflections on Brecht hails theory as the operation of autonomous Dionysian enactment at a moment and its simultaneous codification that, in turn, would enable another such autonomous enactment at another moment. Yet, in spite of that dialectical and allegorical awareness of theory in working-class politics he falls prey to the Heideggerian problem in his own practice where he temporalises the sense of the moment and hypostatises it. It is a problem that is born out of having to defend the logical universality of class politics in a moment of revolutionary retreat, when the antithetical fetishes comprising the various contradictory junctures of a capitalist conjuncture are sought to be overcome by positing the universality of the singular (and synthetic) revolutionary logic. But Adorno ended up positing that universal logic of revolutionary processuality by seeking to pedagogically transmit the conceptualised form, through which he had enacted that logic of critical autonomy in the determinate moment of theory and discursive discourse, on to other concrete moments of capitalist contradiction.

This imposed transmission of the conceptualised form through which the revolutionary logic manifest itself determinately in the moment of theory destroyed the singularity of universality, for real universality is possible only when there is no alienated duality that implies a struggle between competing particulars intrinsic to the horizon of alienated duality. That Adorno pedagogically imposed a conceptualised form of the universality of the one (singular-universal) determinate to a particular moment on other moments is evident in his theory of negative dialectics that sees every act of resistance, the moment it is enunciated, as being antithetical and thus governed and articulated by the capitalist logic of competing fetishes. His negative dialectics displaces the synthetic process so completely into the domain of the absent that he cannot ever distinguish between the symptomally materialised critique of the total system in a local moment of its appearance from the fetish it is destined to become in the next moment. His *negative dialectics, in fact, has no place for envisaging power or dialectics in their determinate materiality*. To that extent, *his vision robs the dialectical logic of the materiality that Marx had conferred on it while rescuing it from the distortions of Hegel's teleologised and phenomenologised prison.*

It is no wonder then that Adorno always sees the importance of a form in terms of what it cannot say. He, thanks to his negative dialectical vision, cannot ever see that a form, in the moment of its critical emergence, vis-à-vis another ontologically fixed form that affirms its logic of form as such thereby establishing duality, domination and externalised pedagogical determination, is enunciated in the realm of the positive even before it can become a form there. The figuring of such an enunciative register in the realm of the positive shows that the unalienated logic of the singular processual, which is the logical inverse of ontologised forms and their formal logic of domination and duality, can and does appear in the positive by breaking with the ontologically fixed forms and their logic of alienation, duality, contradiction and domination. *The melancholy Marxist, as a consequence, could never see what a form says in terms of how and why it says so. His negative dialectics, wherein the synthetic always resides in the elsewhere of the negative and the absent, actually implies that this elsewhere of synthetic negativity appears only in the mental moment of human thought.* The hypostatisation of the form in which the processual synthetic logic appeared in a determinate fashion to the mental-theoretical moment, something that was built into Adorno's temporalisation of the sense of the theoretical moment of class struggle, made it impossible for him to envisage the unfolding of the processual synthetic logic, which was constitutive of the form of critique determinate to the mental-theoretical moment, through its repeated determinate re-enactment in the specificity of other moments of capitalist duality and contradiction. It was this that led Adorno's theoretical practice in the direction of radical negativity that precluded all revolutionary hope and made optimism of the will an impossibility.

Adorno, even while being critically enactive in the theoretical moment of institutionalised academics, turns pedagogical in taking the conceptualised form of that enactment rather literally with regard to other moments, especially the moment of political pragmatics, of capitalist duality and contradiction.

That now brings us to Althusser. His project of doing philosophy under the condition of politics gave us a revolutionary and mobile 'metaphysics' that obviated his theory's pedagogical reception, and made the re-enactment and refoundation of the logic of unalienated processuality, which was constitutive of his form of critique in the moment of theory and canonical philosophy, inescapable. *Althusser's defence of the revolutionary horizon—as it is encapsulated in a conceptually elevated form through which critique and the coeval logic of unalienated processuality were enacted at the moment of philosophy—is simultaneously a call for re-enactment.* The fact that they are not discrete ideas renders Althusser, Zizek and Badiou's notion of philosophy as anti-dialogic combat quasi-Stalinist, a stance that working-class politics would do well to adopt today.

4

The Siren Songs of Neo-traditionalism

Maxim Gorky's Leninist assertion "Aesthetics is the ethics of future" has been a key obsession of both Jean-Luc Godard's cinematic oeuvre and his theoretical reflections on cinema. This indicates a preoccupation that can hardly be termed capricious. An obsessive concern with the twin conceptions of aesthetics and ethics, which has preponderantly animated the discourse and engagements of the cultural left in all its multifarious shades, has emerged out of a rather grave predicament that has not been its alone. It began, at least as far as our modern (or postmodern) times go, ever since Søren Kierkegaard decided to give conceptual flesh to the idea of aesthetics and reformulate it.

Kierkegaard's encounter with the degrading march of history, post Industrial Revolution, pushed him towards Catholicism and led him to conceive of aesthetics as a form of *intuitive* and *non-reflective* knowledge that has absolutely nothing to do with lived history, its ethical universe and the contemplative and critical knowledge that is acquired or produced by engaging with this objective world. For the Danish philosopher, the ethic of capitalism dehumanised man whose only "redemption" was in freeing his subjectivity from its entanglements with history and turning it inwards. What Kierkegaard's hasty rebellion against the brutalising ethics of capitalism missed was that subjectivity can never be free of the existing objective conditions. His unwillingness, or inability, to locate his own 'rebellion of faith' in the objective context of his time—that is, in failing to perceive that his 'aesthetic' revolt was necessitated by the 'ethical' world of capitalism—only allowed the dehumanising juggernaut to roll on unhindered as he prepared to make his "leap of faith". That, in short, is the tale of how aesthetics floundered into the blind alley of inwardness and inaction. And it is precisely this blind alley from where Godard, following in Gorky's Leninist foolsteps, has attempted to rescue aesthetics by setting up a dialogic confrontation between the self and the world. Contrary to what Kierkegaard would have us believe, human subjectivity and all its motions always occur within what he called the "ethical universe". Therefore, the self, even when it turns inwards, is choosing to respond to the larger dynamic of objective history in a particular fashion. The failure to recognise this relationship between the 'subjectivity' of aesthetics and the 'objective' realm of ethics, compels us to eschew all possibilities of struggling against and in the world to change it. The end of human suffering, in such a scenario, becomes an illusive, otherworldly affair.

Kierkegaard might be dead and gone but his spectre continues to haunt the quotidian world of human struggles, one that is programmed to seek 'profane' resolutions for this-worldly sufferings. The Kierkegaardian delusion of an unproblematised and free human subjectivity has surfaced time and again in the history of ideas and has afflicted even Marxists, who claim to have their noses deep in objective history. In our day and age, this trend is best represented by that peculiarly postcolonial discourse of subalternity and neo-traditionalism. And the protagonists in this theatre of discourse, in spite of the exhilarating expanse of their discourse and the noble adventure of their ideas, have not been astute enough to realise how Kierkegaard's shadow looms large over them. Their attempts to develop the much-needed critique of a positivistic conception of science and Indian Marxism, which they correctly claim is completely overwhelmed by positivism, show how they have erred on the side of philosophical speculation only to succumb to the temptations of allowing the idea of free and unproblematised human subjectivity to inform much of their theorisation.

One can hardly quibble with, for instance, an Ashish Nandy, when he insists on the need to develop a critique of the domination of modern scientific discourse by positivism. None, least of all perceptive Marxists, can deny assertions that the rift between the observed and the observer, so central to positivistic science, has dominated human consciousness ever since Francis Bacon and his idea of inductive knowledge. But all that ought to have changed, at least in the domain of natural sciences, with Einstenian relativity, quantum mechanics, Heisenberg's uncertainty principle and the anthropic cosmological principle shattering the notion that reality of the observed world was a thing in itself and was independent of how the observer perceived it. But that, as we know, has done little to change the dominant scientific discourse. And the reason is not far to be found. That all scientific scrutiny should studiously skirt the observing subject is a notion that serves capitalism fine for it precludes all possibility of an epistemology/praxis of historical transcendence and thus helps maintain the prevalent mode of production and its attendant social relations. That is as far as positivism goes. As for Kantian criticality and the rational subject, that has been the other ideology of capitalism. Though the rational subject in Kant is the source of all knowledge—unlike in positivism where the objective world is where all knowledge resides—its rationality is metaphysically given and has no basis in concrete historical-material context of its time. The subject, in both instances, is unlocated and thus unproblematised.

What is, however, even more distressing is that Marxist political praxis here, as in much else of the world, has also been a victim of this positivistic reification. The Stalinist bureaucracies that most Indian communist parties have become, have enabled positivism and/or metaphysical aprioriism to worm its way into the heart of their theory and practice. The organic and dialectical link between theory and the working class has snapped. That is precisely the reason why many of our so-called Marxists attempt to polemicise against the practitioners of the discourse of neo-traditionalist postcolonialism by naively claiming that communist political practice rectifies the problem of bourgeois science by putting it in the service of the proletariat, as if that was enough to fundamentally transform the bourgeois-positivistic scientific discourse and gaze. But the problem in the neo-traditionalist and subalternist discourses begins to show when the critique of positivistic and scientistic Marxism those discourses articulate seek to underscore the failure of Marxists to embrace subaltern (read folk), traditional and even mystical subject positions, a la Gandhi and Tagore. Something that, according to the neo-traditionalist and subalternist prescriptions, would free Indian Marxism from its positivistic hypostatisation. What such discourses are perhaps incapable of realising is that there is a difference between positivistic reification of Marxist praxis and Marxist science per se, and that Marxism needs neither to disclaim its 'Eurocentric' provenance nor fall back on Tagore and Gandhi to cleanse itself of its reifications. Of course, subcontinental Marxist praxis has to be rooted in its native reality, and for that, one will need to engage with not only Gandhi and Tagore, but such other indigenous thinkers and political practitioners as Jotirao Phule, Ramakrishna, Chaitanya, et al. But such an engagement would have to be one of critical assimilation that will seek to problematise not only the subjective positions of such pre-Independence figures, but also those that are located in certain recent currents of indigenist conceptual history that have been trying to foreground, even privilege, and thus rearticulate the subjectivities embodied by those historical personae. That, needless to say, would have to be done by locating both sets of subjectivities in their historical-material and, thus, ideological conjuncture.

It must be emphasised at the outset that the idea of Marxist praxis and the notion of organicity inherent in it is the spirit that will govern such a hermeneutic engagement.

Therefore, what needs to be clarified right at the outset is that this Marxist hermeneutic is not an analytic of interpretation, which claims 'universal scientific' superiority by situating itself in the matrix of conventional positivism, but is a universalising science, precisely because it is self-reflexively aware of its partisan (read proletarian) location. To set apart such an endeavour from metaphysical and/or positivistic polemical protestations, which routinely emanate from our present-day Stalinist party structures, one needs to take recourse to Althusser and his idea of the epistemological break in Marx. Althusser's "Early Marx" is a Feurbachian humanist or, in the language of Late Marx, a "contemplative materialist" for whom the sensuous human subject, as opposed to the abstract subject of Kant and Hegel, is the source of all knowledge. Althusser calls this discourse of unproblematised human subjectivity ideological and sees a rupture separating the scientific historical-materialist position of Late Marx from this earlier discourse. But this Althusserian view of science is not universal as such in its conceptuality. For, that would imply it is located within the hegemonic bourgeois scientific discourse, which would hardly enable it to set itself apart from what the French Marxist calls ideology. For Althusser, the historical materialism of Late Marx, precisely in being premised on the self-reflexive awareness of its own class origins (the praxis of becoming proletarian) – which in a dialectical movement simultaneously enables it to discern and express the different class origins of all other discourses and subject-positions — becomes a science in an entirely new sense. Althusser's Marxist science, therefore, is a discourse that, unlike the bourgeois conception of science, recognises the historical location of all subjectivities, even its own. His theoretical inquiry clearly shows that systems of signification in all structures of thought—including those of Early Marx and Late Marx—are dialectically determined or governed by an "ideological (or counter-ideological) field". It is the change in this field that reconfigures the entire system of signification or structure of a discourse.

Althusser explains the epistemological rupture in Marx as a transformation in the latter's "modality of reflection" brought about by the change in the ideological field within which the two thinking beings (Early Marx and Late Marx) were situated. The counter-ideological field of proletarian praxis, according to Althusser, ensured that class struggle occupied the central place in the discourse of historical materialism and was no longer merely an idea arrived at—like in the Feurbachian Early Marx—while trying to solve the 'central' riddle of human alienation. Marx, in settling his account with his earlier Young Hegelian phase through the realisation that man and his thought were located in a specific historical conjuncture and thus could not be envisaged as unproblematised and fixed ontic and epistemic entities, experienced how his own thought had a social basis in the proletarian class struggles of his day. This awareness of the social location of one's own thought is, if Althusser is to be believed, the Marxist conception of partisan science that seeks to universalise itself by organising and conducting its own class struggle.

In fact, Marx's realisation that a being and its thought are determined by their place within an ideological, and thus political-economic, matrix is most clearly evident in his *Theses on Feurbach.* In the second thesis, Marx writes: "The question whether objective truth can be attributed to human thinking is not a question of theory but is a practical question. Man must prove the truth, i.e., the reality and power, the this-worldliness of his thinking in practice. The dispute over the reality or non-reality of thinking which is isolated from practice is a purely *scholastic* question."

This pointedly anti-positivistic (and anti-anthropologistic) impulse of Marx is what guides his and Engels' idea of "scientific" socialism and distinguishes it from bourgeois conceptions of the same, which the duo had decided to call "utopian". The scientific/utopian dichotomy is thus not, as many of its indigenist Indian critics believe, the result of Marx and Engels being the children of the bourgeois Enlightenment with its predominantly positivistic ethos. The break with it is, as a matter of fact, more than evident. In his fifth thesis on Feurbach, Marx writes: "Feurbach, not satisfied with *abstract thinking,* wants [*sensuous*] *contemplation;* but he does not conceive sensuousness as practical, human-sensuous activity."

It is precisely this inability to comprehend the anti-positivistic scientific spirit of Marxism that leads intellectuals such as Nandy to conflate the aprioriism (and/or positivism) apparent in the political practice of the present-day communist parties with the "scientific socialism" of Marx and Engels. In fact, their inability or unwillingness to discover in "scientific socialism" the antidote to positivistic ideological contamination of current Marxist praxis compels them to suggest that Marxism has a lesson or two to learn from certain indigenous subaltern notions of experience, time, struggle, authority and knowledge.

Of course, as has been stated earlier, subcontinental Marxists need to engage in a dialogue with such indigenous discourses. But what will perhaps set such dialogic encounters apart from the *subalternist* enterprise is the acknowledgement, that these indigenous subaltern discourses, in spite of their pre-capitalistic and pre-modern origins, are accessed today through the various avenues created by capitalism and its culture of bourgeois modernity. The fact that these 'subaltern' discourses come to us, for instance, through the market, underscores their commodification and thus the historical transformation of their use value by their exchange value that is unlocked by their entry into the world of capitalism. To take a rather simplistic example, the various animist myths and their associated representations were, in their own pre-capitalistic political economies, a way of making sense of the world around and were accessed as such. Today, these representations have been transformed into tribal craft as they have entered the market and have been monetised and are accessed (or consumed) like commodities. That is, they are no longer merely technologies that their respective animist social orders employ to make sense of nature and the world around, but are also seen for their 'beauty' as handicraft and the anthropological knowledge they can provide about their own societies. Their producers are no longer tribal shamans, mystics or witch doctors, but are proletarian artisans. This has been due to the fact that their pre-capitalist modes of production have not remained as such and the universalising and irruptive monetisation brought about by the capitalist mode of production has transformed their knowledge-systems into commodities.

The *subalternists* can, of course, still argue that monetisation need not completely change the various subaltern modes of existence and that their discourses, myths and their various notions of non-linear pre-modern time continue to govern their lives. What must, however, be perceived is that these pre-capitalistic technologies have undergone transformation and have become ideological, simply because the pre-capitalist modes of production, within which they were conceived, have been monetised and have become the margins of an industrial-capitalist system. For instance, the idea of timelessness, which our subalternist and neo-traditionalist intellectuals uphold and celebrate, is the product of a mode of production that has ceased to be and survives only in its ideological forms. Many agrarian and tribal communities still follow the seasonal and circular conception of time, once in vogue in this geo-civilisational mass called the Indian subcontinent, but the real time that now governs their life is the calendar of the modern capitalist market where they have to either sell their produce or their labor-power, or the former as the embodiment of the latter. They are no longer peasants inhabiting a feudal mode of production or the member of a hunter-gatherer or pastoral tribe, but are the proletariat in the market and society of modern capitalism. Their stubborn reluctance to grasp this, say in their dogged refusal to give up their pre-capitalistic conception of circular time, is nothing short of false consciousness. Their real subalternity, in such a situation, is their proletarian status, not some pre-capitalistic way of life, which is an ideological remnant now only serving to conceal and obscure their real status from them and thus preventing their *expression* and *empowerment* as a class for itself. The Marxists—unlike subalternists—will, in the process of dialectically engaging with such pre-capitalistic ideological 'subalternities' lay bare the process of how capitalism and monetisation have transformed their 'original' subalternities into the *subalternity of the present* (our current history).

What needs to be asked at this juncture is: what keeps many intellectuals and scholars, especially of this postcolonialist, indigenist vintage, from perceiving this *subalternity of the present?* Or, why does their discourse end up reifying subalternity? More importantly, what is it that stops them from recognising this theoretical failing of theirs? The answer can probably be located in the ideological matrix within which their discourse is circumscribed. It is here that creative Marxists should try and expand their understanding of ideology. An ideology, since it is produced, is also a product. In fact, it is more than that—it creates not only itself but also its channels of access. In short, what needs to be seen is the dialectic between ideologies, and the modes of production and relations of production they help maintain and perpetuate. An ideology emanates from a certain mode of production, but by virtue of being a product of that mode it is also produced and consumed by the mechanisms of production and consumption of that mode of production.

An ideological apparatus, a la Althusser, which helps maintain and reproduce the capitalist mode of production, is disseminated through the distribution channels created by the market and it is, therefore, also a commodity. Its use value as an ideology is determined by its exchange value as a commodity and vice-versa. That is, an ideology creates and reproduces an economy and the economy makes that ideology available as a commodity. Any counter-ideological discourse or impulse in the age of capitalism disseminated through its market is commodified and is thus, in the ultimate analysis, unable to be counter-ideological vis-a-vis capitalism and its ethos of commodity fetishism. That is the heart of the problem embodied by our neo-traditionalist intellectuals. Their entire discourse, in spite of all its noble intentions, is created and accessed within the context of the bourgeois academia and the publishing market. In short, they are firmly entrenched within the capitalist mode of production and are governed by its logic.

Walter Benjamin says in his 'The Author as Producer' that the more important question for him, than asking what is the attitude of a work to the mode of production of its time, is "...'What is its position in them?' This question directly concerns the function the work has within the literary relations of production of its time. It is concerned in other words, directly with the literary (technique) of the works." This idea of technique, as Benjamin correctly points out, made intellectual and artistic creations accessible to a materialist analysis and thus enabled revolutionary intellectuals to visualise ideology in its totality—as a product and therefore governed by the laws of its mode of production. Thus it is Benjamin again who endorses Brecht's position and says that he "was the first to make of intellectuals the far-reaching demand not to supply the apparatus of production without to the utmost extent possible, changing it in accordance with socialism". Brecht's *Umfunktionierung*, or functional transformation, of the mode of production within which revolutionary intellectuals produce their politically revolutionary and aesthetically avant-garde work, is actually linked to the very process of production and distribution. An intellectual unaware of his location within his mode of production is one whose subjectivity is congealed and unproblematised and whatever he produces, no matter how revolutionary and counter-hegemonical its intent, will, in the final reckoning, be contained and coopted.

Benjamin provides an instance:"...we are faced with the fact—of which the past decade (mid-1920s to mid-1930s) in

Germany has furnished an abundance of examples—that the bourgeois apparatus of production and publication can assimilate astonishing quantities of revolutionary themes, indeed, can propagate them without calling its own existence, and the existence of the class that owns it, seriously into question." The consumer-producer split, which is the very basis of the capitalist mode of production, is what gives rise to, and is serviced by the pre-Marxian idea of the contemplative intellectual. *Functionally transforming* this mode of production means that the producer-consumer rift be done away with and every intellectual creation is such that it is not passively consumed but is a form of inspiring and organising people along class lines to be a part of the mode of production that enables the creation of this intellectual product. That is, to join in the class struggle.

The postcolonial indigenist discourses of academically canonised human sciences remains at the level of a metadiscourse of reified subalternities because it steers clear of the idea of "scientific socialism" and class struggle. As a result, it also fails to recognise its own position within the given mode of intellectual production (the bourgeois academia and the publishing market) and fails to problematise its own subjectivity. Consequently, the proponents of such discourses turn out to be the best exemplars of contemplative materialism, nothing more, and nothing less. Marx writes in his ninth thesis on Feurbach: "The highest point reached by contemplative materialism, that is materialism which does not comprehend sensuousness as practical activity, is the contemplation of single individuals and of civil society." Therefore, the result of their unproblematised and non-proletarianised subjectivity is voluntarism, which leads them to believe they can intervene at the level of 'civil society' by taking 'counter-hegemonical' positions. The pedagogically interventionist writings and lectures of these contemplative materialists, who claim to be articulating a traditionalist and indigenist critique of western science and Marxism, are peppered with instances of ideologically unlocated *human* individuals intervening and setting things right in the sphere of education, civil rights and other segmented arms of the 'civil society'.

For instance, sociologist Avijit Pathak, who claims to share Nandy's ground of indigenist critique of positivist and 'Eurocentric' modernity and who also derives heavily from the conceptual apparatus and logic of the Subaltern Studies school, is of the opinion that a radical arithmetic teacher in the classroom of an elite bourgeois school can make a lot of difference by his 'different' methodology of teaching and radicalise a few of his students. He may be right but that process of radicalisation will be chancy to say the least and will be superficial and normative at best. For a paradigm shift in the field of education, it is important to realise the context and the mode of production within which such bourgeois schools operate and the limitations of their classrooms as far as complete radicalisation is concerned. For, the counter-hegemonical knowledge, which a few teachers might want to disseminate in a bourgeois classroom that is the agency for distributing the commodity of education, can only be consumed and can hardly give rise to a context within which students also become producers and the teacher-taught distinction is abolished.

So, voluntarism is a generous impulse only insofar as it enables the voluntarist to see its limitations, compelling him to find a way of transcending it. Revolutionary practice, according to Lenin, is impossible without a revolutionary theory. The question that one needs to ask today is: what will revolutionary theory serve if there is no revolutionary practice? Thus pedagogy, for a Marxist, can only be a conceptual part of his political praxis and cannot be tackled in isolation. Any attempt to do so is either bound to fail gloriously or be coopted. Examples of such failures abound. And the blame lies not merely at the doorsteps of such civil rights and pedagogical groups as Eklavya, but also the sundry communist parties, which have failed to create a revolutionary praxis that could have constellationally integrated such attempts. The result is that Eklavya's Hoshangabad Science Teaching programme—with its radical pedagogical techniques of imparting science education to villagers without the benefit of established laboratories—had to be run under the patronage of the Madhya Pradesh government, which could capriciously decide to dispense with it.

Same has been the fate of the Visva Bharati University, Shantiniketan. Set up by Tagore to give wings to his idea of the doing-student, it is today, as is often disparagingly called the "UGC's Visva Bharati"; a provincialised Bengali ghetto. What most fail to notice is that the problems of Visva Bharati are located in Tagore's ideas and their historical conjuncture and context. No critical engagement with one's lineage can be complete without the awareness of a historical materialist. And it is on that count that Nandy, the foremost indigenist advocate of Tagore, and his epigones fail in their engagement with the poet.

They extol Tagore's idea of assimilating Santhal, Baul and other folk forms in his music, art and, most important of all, his pedagogical conceptions, but fail to notice that the 'folk' does not express itself but is represented by art, which by itself has a certain historical-materialist provenance. The artistic gaze and the aesthetic sensibility, as we all know, is a product of the European Renaissance and the humanising impulse of an ascendant bourgeoisie. Creations and representations outside that spatio-temporal and/or ideological framework served an altogether different purpose and created absolutely different sensibilities from what we encounter in the domain of art today. For instance, folk forms in India or pre-Renaissance 'art' were religious in nature and were tied to the feudal or pre-capitalist communitarian idea of collectivities and the collective gaze. Thus individual styles, whenever there were any, were absorbed and made a part of the larger collective or guild. This had to do with the largely homogeneous perception of religious hierarchies within and between collectivities. The birth of the artist and his individual style is linked to the freedom of individual interpretation and humanisation that accompanied the rise of industrial capitalism with its emphasis on individual enterprise. This opened up many possibilities of looking at the world and created the ideology of the free artistic spirit by fracturing the homogeneities of the pre-capitalist world. In such a scheme of things, in which free artistic spirit and the multiplicities of looking at and representing realities are actually the consequence of a laissez-faire of the artistic commodities, pre-capitalistic representations became craft as opposed to art, and their creators, artisans as opposed to artists.

Tagore's whole idea of empowering and representing the artisan and his craft was to provide space for him within art as it was constituted within a bourgeois discourse. The subaltern, as is his wont, could not empower himself and was *re-presented.* This formed the basis of not only Tag ore's own creative pursuits, but also that of Shantiniketan. The doing student, whom Tagore had intended to produce in this 'cradle of new education', failed to find a context in the Nehruvian nation-state and the "mixed economy" it fostered. The resultant take-over of the university by the UGC is only the symptom of this larger problem.

In Tagore's ideas, critical engages can discern germs of an epic struggle. *The Crisis of Civilisation (Sabhyatar Sankat)* is an epitome of that struggle. Widely cited by intellectuals such as Nandy and Pathak, the text of this lecture delivered by Tagore on the occasion of his 80th birthday stresses upon the crisis of the Anglophone civilisation. Tagore dwells at length on his own disillusionment with the liberal project of the English civilisation and locates all the contemporary ills of imperialism, war and colonial subjugation in it. Thus one can read *The Crisis...* as an indictment of liberalism and its interdependence with imperialism and the expansion of capital. But Tagore's complete reliance on the concept of civilisation—and the way he attributes the then Soviet Russia's or Japan's or Iran's prosperity to some superior, inclusivist civilisational vision that managed to accommodate all sections of their respective societies and harmonise them—

obscures the truth and sometimes misrepresents it. The prosperity in Soviet Union then, for instance, was the result of a proletarian political praxis and an organic building of the CPSU. It was certainly not the result of some overarching civilisational paradigm that made space for various subaltern nationalities (like the "nomadic Muslim ethnicities" of the Central Asian republic) and communities. If we are not able to see the initial Soviet success in these terms, the latter-day Stalinist excesses and the manipulation of the nationalities by a party that had been fetishised by its complete alienation from the working class it claimed to represent will make absolutely no sense. Similarly, in case of Japan and Iran, his civilisational paradigm prevented him from explaining the violence that these two societies concealed deep within themselves. And though this critique of Anglophone liberalism and its influence on exclusivist discourse of Indian nationalism and nationhood can be seen as Tagore's geo-civilisational alternative to ideas of nationhood and nationalism, today, in face of the rising Hindu Right, they can only be made effective if they are redefined within the revolutionary praxis of the working class. Otherwise, they can only be contained and coopted along with their modern-day upholders and their metadiscourse of reified subalternities.

Artist Abanindranath Tagore's view of art, which prospered in his uncle's Shantiniketan, is actually an excellent indication of how the radical notions of pedagogy, folk and craft in Visva Bharati were limited and contained by the ideological conjuncture from which they sprang. Abanindranath, in his "The Prodigals of Art' (*'Shilpay Anadhikar' in Bageshwari Shilpa Prabandhabali*) bemoans the loss of the artistic sensibility and looks forward to the day when the whole of this land will once again be able to rightfully inherit what is its own—great art like the Taj Mahal and the Ajanta frescoes. He blames the "ugliness in our lives" on "cinema and football". He really wanted to take art to all and sundry and recreate beauty in their lives. The point is he did not succeed, not even in and around Shantiniketan where the Santhals and the Bauls have been progressively pauperised.

High art (*shilpa*) has always been the realm of counter-ideological experiences within capitalism. Yet, capitalism has managed to tame it by cutting the realm off from the lived experience of the people. In Adorno's opinion, the mass culture-high art dichotomy created by capitalism's ideological discourse severs art from the experience of the masses. The exchange value of a work of art in the market is determined, as Adorno points out, precisely by its "uselessness", in utilitarian terms of the capitalist mode of production in its so-called civil society. The aura of something more than usefulness has to be shattered and the valorisation of the artistic spirit, which is nothing more than a kind of commodity fetishism, has to end before everybody starts accessing art. However, a mode of production, which thrives on the creation of surplus value and in which art too has to serve that end, can hardly afford to do away with these reifications—of the mysterious and mystical artistic spirit—that only serve to increase the exchange value of the art-products. So, you have Abanindranath wishing that everyone accesses art, but is unwilling to shatter its aura, which will make that possible. In his 'The Prodigals...' the difference between the artist and the artisan is that between the honeybee and the wasp. "Both their hives are similar, the only difference is that there are honeycombs in the former's hive where sweet honey is made and we don't know how. That is art!" He presses the point further when he says that the artist's work is *"nirmiti"* (creation) as opposed to *"nirman"* (construction) in case of the artisan. The privileging of the 'mysterious' artistic spirit is complete.

Unless one is able to distinguish between the noble intentions of the two Tagores and the location of their thought in the ideological conjuncture of their time, which created a contradiction between intent and practice, one cannot ever hope to creatively engage with them and will only end up putting them on display in reified museums of the present.

5

Akhtaruzzaman Elias: Beyond The Lived Time of Nationhood

> "And to say now that you are no longer here is to say only that you have entered a different order of things, in that the one we move in here, we latecomers, as insane as it is, seems to our way of thinking the only one in which "god" can spread out all of his possibilities, become known and recognized within the framework of an assumption whose significance we do not understand."
>
> — From **Eugenio Montale's** 'Visit to Fadin'

Introduction

If there is a time for everything, there must be a time for revolution too. But revolutionary time can often become its own time-warp. It can freeze one moment, among many, of revolutionary politics into its eternalised truth and thus prevent such politics from recognising the new moments of revolutionary reality that lie beyond the moment it has mystified as its be-all. Concomitantly, such mystification also prevents it from realising its own potential. This potential can be sensed and expressed only when revolutionary politics is driven by the will to relentlessly transcend its various moments to constantly encounter itself within different possible historical temporalities. Alas, it is the South Asian Left more than any other, either in the 'Third' or 'First' World, that has been the worst victim of this historical time freeze. A self-containing, even psychotic, numbness, which goes by the name of national anti-colonial resistance, has held South Asian 'revolutionary' praxis in its tightly malignant grip for the past five decades. The upshot: it still articulates its politics in terms of the nation—preponderantly, in the idiom of national sovereignty and independence.

Clearly, its understanding of revolutionary politics continues to be haunted by the spectres of its origins, which lie in a 'third world' conjunctural complex of national-liberation struggles against direct colonialism on the one hand and 'socialist' struggles against neo-colonialism on the other. The failure of the South Asian Left, particularly its Indian strand, to posit its politics shorn of all idioms of national independence, and in classical Marxist terms of class struggle *per se*, must be ascribed to its cussed refusal to acknowledge the fact that imperialism as a phenomenon has long outgrown its colonial (or neo-colonial) moment of oppressive politico-economic occupation of foreign lands.

It is in this context that Bangladeshi writer Akhtaruzzaman Elias's politico-aesthetic framework, especially the way he expounded it through his novels *Khowabnama* (Dream Chronicle) and *Chilekotar Sepai* (The Soldier in the Attic), acquires immense importance. The praxis of cultural politics that this framework adumbrates would, if adopted by the South Asian Left, open up new pathways of resistance and revolution beyond the confines of its stale and stifling national-liberation paradigm. The attempt here is to envisage the politico-aesthetic vision of the Bangladeshi author, together with that of filmmaker Ritwik Ghatak's, as an integral part of an exiguous though crucial ideological strain within what may provisionally be called the Bengali Left. The fundamental politico-aesthetic impulse of Elias and Ghatak's art, and their stance on the political in general, could be constitutive of a new politics of resistance that is free from the vicissitudes of the national-liberation paradigm.

Paradigms of Revolution or Prisons of Reaction

We will truly appreciate the pressing need for such a praxis when we fully reckon with the incalculable damage South

Asian Left's near complete dependence on idioms of national independence/sovereignty has done to its struggle against imperialism. Its reliance on this outdated paradigm to understand, critique and intervene in the current politico-economic situation has prevented it from coming to grips with the new moment of "imperialism without colonies".

That has not only rendered the Left here incapable of formulating its anti-imperialist struggle—now more a shibboleth than a critical vision of politics—as anti-capitalism, it has also sapped our comrades of all capacity to accurately diagnose the reason behind the degeneration of the originally progressive national-liberation projects of their respective societies into jingoistic authoritarianisms and/or reactionary fascisms. It would do its purported politics of anti-imperialism a whole load of good if the Left were to accept the fact that we are now part of a decentred empire of various nationally deterritorialised capitals competing with one another. Its inadequate and ineffectual response to the rising tide of fascisms and various other forms of reactionary identity politics in this part of the world must, to complete the dialectic of haplessness, be blamed on its stubborn persistence with the timeworn frameworks and categories of national liberation.

Much of its supposed critique of fascism, as a result, is embedded in and imbued by categories of bourgeois ethics and liberal modernity, which prove ineffective precisely because they fail to zero in on the political-economic essence or logic of fascism. Fascism has to be located as a problem of the larger socio-economic structure, of which liberal modernity, bourgeois ethics of secularism and imperialism are constitutive elements. For instance, the Indian Left's programmatic attempt to pose 'secular' and 'economic' nationalism against, simultaneously, the 'cultural nationalism' of RSS-BJP-type fascist forces and 'western' imperialism shows it is completely oblivious to the political economy of the nation-state. Such nationalistic anti-imperialism has not only weakened its struggle against the national component of global-imperialist capital, it has not in any essential sense enabled the Left to critique fascism because it shares with the fascists, particularly of the Hindutva variety, the same structural and logical premises (nation, nationalism, national pride etc) of politics. All that the various strains of the Indian Left have done so far by way of resisting the Hindutva forces is load those categories with a superficially different ethical or normative charge. Not surprisingly, all those leftist strains have without exception been condemned to fight fascism on the latter's terms and turf. They have, we have, failed grievously to posit any structural alternative to the current political-economic order that fosters fascism and imperialism as dialectical halves of one single phenomenon: "globalisation".

Elias and Ghatak: New And Different Pathways

It is in the backdrop of globalisation that the significance of Elias and Ghatak's conceptions of art, aesthetics and politics must be fully unfolded and grasped. Both the writer and the filmmaker, separated by almost a generation and national boundaries, were critical of the national-liberation paradigm, particularly in the context of Bangladesh's struggle for independence.

They both recognised, and depicted through their art, the obfuscatory and obstructionist nature of that paradigm, vis-à-vis the essential project of social revolution. Yet, more important and interesting than this similarity of their critiques is the difference in their politico-aesthetic register and orientation. Elias's critique of the national liberation/nationhood paradigm is, thanks to this difference, more fundamentally anti-systemic. There is absolutely no doubt that the social revolutionary aspirations of the urban underclass, poor peasantry and radical intelligentsia of Bengali East Pakistan—against the expropriative and exploitative machinations of the West Pakistani elite, its Rawalpindi-based military executive and their local agents—was the trigger of the national liberation struggle that erupted with the "Bhasha Andolan" (language movement) of 1952. Elias has shown as much in *Sepai*. But what is equally true is that linguistic-cultural (Bengali) nationalism was, in terms of this elemental social revolutionary impulse, a unifying local ideological idiom of resistance. Especially since West Pakistani colonialism played itself out in East Pakistan in Punjabi racist and anti-Bengali terms. Considering that this colonialism—a local extractive moment of the global political economy of imperialist capital—was held together in the name of a Muslim national brotherhood by a ruling class consisting of West Pakistanis and a sizeable chunk of East Bengalis, this idiom of Bengali nationalism was, to begin with, useful. Ultimately, however, Bengali chauvinism subsumed and subverted the fundamental social revolutionary impulse of the national-liberation struggle of Bangladesh. A fact noted and critically depicted by both Ghatak and Elias in their cinema and literature respectively.

In Ghatak's last film, *Jukti, Takko ar Gappo* (Logic, Argument and Story), protagonist Neelkantha, Ghatak's alter ego, deliberately severs himself from the general sense of nostalgia for a united Bengal rampant among the petty-bourgeois intellectuals of Calcutta-centric Indian West Bengal. What may seem surprising is that Ghatak/Neelkantha—despite his exilic yearning for a lost idyll and the concomitant dream of a West Bengal reconciled with east—does not share the petty-bourgeois optimism in vogue in contemporary West Bengal about the power of the linguistic-nationalist liberation struggle to achieve real reconciliation.

In fact, he violently rejects such optimism. His rejection embodies not only the impossibility of the fulfilment of this fantasy, but also its undesirability. This sensibility is, in a certain sense, classically Marxian as its expression is at one and the same time ethical and political. For Neelkantha (and Ghatak), the unity of Bengal is not merely about the overcoming of a superficial religious (Hindu-Muslim) divide to reconcile a linguistically-culturally 'similar' people.

It is also about accentuating the various inflection points between reified 'conventional' and elitist (*bhadralok*) Bengali culture and various 'little' cultures dotting the Bengal-Bihar-Orissa continuum.

It is Ghatak's conception of a more dialogic, organic and composite Bengaliness that drives him, through Neelkantha, to accentuate those inflection points. But such Bengaliness is only a cultural epiphenomenon of something much more essential. The premise of Ghatak's vision, in contrast to the petty-bourgeois culturalist perspective of 'one Bengal', is political-economic. Ghatak seeks to underscore the reification of modern Bengaliness and, in the process, points out the political-economic logic of production of territorialised and stratified cultural differences. It must, however, be mentioned that Ghatak's vision is informed as much by his encounter with a Marxist critique of capitalist political economy as it is rooted in the non- and pre-Renaissance cultural sensibility of Bengal. This sensibility of Atish Dipankar (a 10th-11th century Buddhist monk from Bengal) and Chaitanya, who pre-date the so-called Bengal Renaissance, was borne forward by figures such as Ramakrishna Paramahansa and even partially Rabindranath Tagore during the Renaissance. (It must be stated as an aside that Tagore, contrary to his conventional image, was not a full-fledged Renaissance hat. He was split between the romantic individualism and realism of Renaissance and a self-effacing classicism specific to various communitarianisms in pre-modern Bengal.) Renaissance privileged the modern, knowing subject situated within a telelogically fraught romantic gaze, and thus established the supremacy of knowledge objectified, captured and represented by this gaze. In so doing, it created the fundamental terrritorialised hierarchy between the knowing culture (on top) and the known culture (below it) and served to destroy the composite organicity of pre-Renaissance communities, what with genteel 'Bengaliness' emerging as an alienated, superordinate, and determining centre, vis-à-vis the various 'little' and 'demotic' cultures around it.

But the grounding of Ghatak's critical political-economic prism in a communitarian cultural sensibility leads, not surprisingly, to its contamination. As a result, communitarian organicity does not function merely as the logic of negative dialectical critique of alienation and the political economy of capitalism. Instead, it is ontologised as a lost and transcendental Arcadia. As a result, Ghatak's rejection of culturalist euphoria over the "impending" reconciliation of Bengal ends up denying the sedimented class reality immanent in the Bangladeshi war of national-liberation.

And this is exactly where Elias's political, and aesthetic, approach becomes distinguishable from Ghatak's. Growing up in East Pakistan, the writer has to confront the question of national liberation much more directly. So, while he shares Ghatak's critique of the obfuscatory idiom of national-liberation, once it became the predominant ideological form of articulating resistance in East Pakistan, he does not stop looking for possibilities of social revolution immanent in this form. In *Chilekotar Sepai*, he dwells at length on how the children and grand-children of elite Muslim Leaguers among the local, Bengali-speaking East Pakistani population gradually seized the leadership of the liberation struggle as they saw the tide turn. It also shows how this seizure of leadership was accompanied by an excessive emphasis on Bengali linguistic unity against the Urdu-speaking colonialists of Pakistan, even as the fundamental socio-economic question of the peasantry and working class was first relegated to the background and subsequently suppressed. Such precedence of nationalist Bengali unity over socio-economic transformation served to conceal and repress a very crucial aspect of Pakistani colonialism in East Bengal: the exploitation and oppression of the East Bengali working class and peasantry by the local elite, patronised and protected by Rawalpindi. But the most insightful aspect of the novel, as far as we are concerned, is the legitimacy the Communist Left of East Bengal conferred on this turn of events by slowing down and then withdrawing from the peasant struggles against landlordism in countryside. But this understanding of Elias, which accurately highlights the perils of confronting colonialism as a cultural-linguistic phenomenon, does not impel him to reject the Bangladeshi national liberation struggle in its entirety. Unlike Ghatak, he seeks to foreground the possibilities of social revolution immanent in and repressed by a struggle that has come to be seen as a pure cultural-linguistic movement. The character of underclass Haddi Khijir, whom Elias creates as a counterpoint to Marxist intellectual Anwar and other more cynical upholders of Bengali nationhood—like Khijir's employer Allaudin, nephew and son-in-law of loyal Muslim Leaguer Rahmatullah—is meant to simultaneously emphasise this possibility and its repression.

What foregrounds Elias's search for immanent possibilities of social revolution in the Bangladeshi national-liberation struggle is the last section of *Sepai*, where protagonist Osman Gani, till then an inert inhabitant of the oppressive status quo, locates through his delirious visions the drive, strength and truth of the national-liberation movement in the upsurge of the urban underclass and lumpen-proletariat of East Bengal. That Khijir, shot dead by the Pakistani army, should come to life in Osman's dreams and hallucinations to become a beacon of the national-liberation movement precisely at the moment when the crucial social revolutionary impetus of the liberation struggle is being contained in the name of Bengali linguistic-national unity bears Elias's concerns out. The moment when Osman's delusions force him to deny and withdraw from existential reality and its rationality is as much the moment of his insanity as the point where he acquires a different historical individuality than the one he had till then embodied. This transformation happens through his realignment, albeit delusively, with a new political practice and formation that resists the socially exploitative and politically oppressive reality of existential time. Madness becomes the science of revolution.

Frantz Fanon's assertion that a national-liberation struggle is nothing if it does not become a struggle for social emancipation is, it seems, also Elias's credo. Anti-colonialism is a cry against forcible extraction of surplus value before it is a demand for national-political self-determination. In fact, the search for such self-determination is simultaneously political and socio-economic. Clearly, the question of political power cannot be dealt with in isolation from the question of socio-economic relations. The logic that underlies the creation of a differential hierarchy of identities, whereby the colonising identity determines the destiny (and identity) of the colonised, is the logic of the exchange value-driven political economy of capitalism. It is a logic, which through competition and/or coercion, introduces alienation into a horizontal, non-identitarian flow to produce a differential of political power and/or socio-economic entitlements and thus creates a vertical stratification of *different* identities.

Such focus on the socio-economic logic of both colonialism and anti-colonialism is important because representative democracies, particularly in ex-colonies such as ours, have a way of obscuring this essence by projecting liberation from foreign rule as the end of the search for self-determination. It seems to suggest that colonialist abominations consist entirely of how colonisers go about their business, and not what that business is. They have, in their representation of colonialism, falsely privileged the use of coercive force by our former colonisers over what that force was actually meant to achieve: transfer of value from a certain section of people, who were compelled to give up control over their means of production, to those who took possession of those means either directly or by setting the rules of the market. Such obfuscation, largely structural, is also sometimes wrought through voluntaristic and deliberate propaganda. It is meant to conceal the fact that a change in the form of government does not change the essential political-economic logic or the class character of the state, which continues to play its crucial role of aiding value transfer for capital accumulation. Liberal representative democracy is, therefore, hardly a viable structural alternative to colonialism, or various forms of totalitarianism.

Bourgeois representative democracy, which talks of political equality among voter-individuals even as it leaves the hierarchical socio-economic relations intact, precludes participatory democracy. Democracy, in such a situation, is chimerical and formal because the political-economic logic of representation, which is constitutive of socio-economic stratification, means that people occupying lower stations of the hierarchy would always be *re-presented* by people above them. In other words, their destinies would be determined by people and institutions that stand apart and above them. Structures and institutions will always determine and *re-present* human beings, never the other way round. The only freedom people have is the freedom to choose who will represent them in those institutions. Representative democracy offers them no freedom to change the structural anti-dialogic logic of *re-presentation* that is manifest through and in the institutions of liberal democracy. There can clearly be no true political equality (of liberties) among individuals without an equality of socio-economic entitlements, and vice-versa. The current system, where *egalité* and *liberté* are notionally on a par but where the latter actually has primacy over the former, has to give way to another order. One that is constituted by a collapse of the two attributes into a singularity that Balibar calls *egaliberté.*

Such obfuscation of the social logic of colonialism and, more importantly, national liberation in post-colonial representative democracies should make us even more attentive to the subtleties of Elias's stance on the issue—a national-liberation movement is no more and no less than a moment of social revolution and class struggle. To that extent, the 'nationalist' struggle of East Bengal against its Pakistani colonisers is for him part of a constellation of various such moments in Bengal's temporal history. Those moments may precede or follow each other in lived time, they may also differ from one another in the idioms in which they express themselves or the authorities they confront. But all of them articulate, either unconsciously or self-consciously, a singular, synchronic tendency: transformation of relations of oppression, exploitation and domination to accomplish autonomy and free association. The manner in which Haddi Khijir views an anti-Pakistan procession he also participates in is revealing.

People have started pouring out from the alleys. From the shanty behind the Nabadwip-Basak Lane, a group of 10-15 men in rags and faded jackets come out. Workers from Shamsuddin's bread factory on Panchbhaighat Lane have left behind the comforting warmth of the tandoor to hit the streets. A group of rickshawpullers has emerged from the Hrishikesh Das Road garage.... The procession of human beings keeps growing in the yellowish-black glow of streetlights and a shiver runs down Khijir's spine. He's certain the old residents of the locality have joined them. But he's unafraid. Call them djinns or specters, today everybody has become one with men.... Residents of Ishwar Das Lane come, accompanied by the students of Bani Bhavan College. Lots of boys from the shoemakers' ghetto next to the municipality office are also here.... Khijir's procession is now opposite Victoria Park. The trees in the park nod their heads affirmatively in response to the slogans. Some sepoys of yore descend from the tall palm trees after freeing themselves from the noose. They too will turn right with the procession. (My translation.)

In Khijir's eyes, the procession, a 'real-life' occurrence in the novel, acquires a dream-like texture with various small collectivities from different spatial and occupational locations of 1969 East Pakistan merging into it. As if this weaving together of spatial and occupational differences into a single fabric of the procession were not enough to establish his conception of 'synchronic' history, Elias ties into it a phenomenon which is separated from the immediate anti-Pakistani upsurge by more than a century. The ghosts of sepoys hanged by the British for their participation in the "mutiny" of 1857 descend from the palm trees of Dhaka to join in. The trope of the procession tells us that Elias does not envisage the continuity of all these struggles as various successive stages of a single ascending history with an idyllic telos. The procession is actually a constellation of struggles bound together by the logic of a single social revolution, albeit manifest through different idioms and political forms in different historical times. This logic of class struggle, it must be pointed out, is not foundational in any phenomenological sense but is only so in the sense of a relational logic intrinsic to capitalism.

The social revolutionary essence of national liberation is Elias's constant preoccupation and it figures in *Khowabnama* as well. In this novel he constructs an account of the Partition (in the east), which does not quite square up with the mainstream historical accounts—whether Bangladeshi, Pakistani or Indian—of the event. He shows that even Muslim League's communal nationalism, which was reactionary to begin with, thrived only by drawing sustenance from the radical politics of the Tebhaga movement. The advances made by League's communal-nationalist politics of Pakistan is, as Elias's *Khowabnama* shows, in large measure due to the adoption of Tebhaga's rhetoric by the League. It is no surprise that such rhetoric, given that Tebhaga was a communist-led movement of sharecroppers for firm tenurial security and transformation of the oppressive and exploitative land relations of rural Bengal, had an overt social revolutionary tenor. That was, however, not the only thing the Muslim League of the late 1940s borrowed from Tebhaga. After the retreat of the communists from the movement, the League also got to capitalise on the social disaffection and political anger among the largely poor Muslim peasantry of the region. It, not surprisingly, gave that anger a communal-nationalist turn. We should not forget that the predominantly Muslim landless labourers and sharecroppers in East Bengal gave the movement for Pakistan in that area its crucial mass and strength.

Thus for Elias, national liberation is a dialectic of two moments—a moment of politically expressing social disaffection and class discontent on one hand; and a moment of institutionalisation of nation, reification of national identity and the concomitant repression of the moment of social struggle on the other.

Such a dialectical understanding of national liberation *a la* Elias leaves us with no option but to critically engage with it and other similar identity struggles—neither embrace them fully nor reject them lock, stock and barrel. This engagement should be such that we are able to discern how the idiom (or form) of an identity movement mediates its essence. In other words, when and how does such a movement best express the singular social revolutionary logic embedded in it, and when and how exactly does a movement's identitarian idiom brush it against its essential grain of social revolution by repressing it and distorting its singular expression. For Elias, the idiom of national liberation is important enough not to be rejected. But it is, at the same time, not so significant as to be fully embraced. National liberation is an identitarian moment in the process of social revolution or class struggle. It must, therefore, be recognised as such and then also be dissolved into the process so that the struggle can find its new moment of most accurate expression. In the absence of such awareness, revolutionary politics either risks mistaking such moments for their essential, singular logic (if and when identity politics is fully embraced), or the essential social revolutionary logic itself becomes a particular moment and thereby loses its singular universality (if and when identity politics is completely rejected). In either case, we are left with the triumph of identity, and its logic of congealment through alienation, over the non-identitarian and non-alienated logic of pure becoming. While social revolutionaries will have to pose the logic of pure becoming against the alienating logic of identity formation, this revolutionary operation must be self-reflexively conscious of the fact that identities are as much the various points of appearance of the singular social revolutionary process in its movement through various spatio-temporalities as they are its equally numerous prisons.

The national-liberationist form of the 1969-71 movement in East Pakistan is, in *Sepai,* important to the extent that it is only through this form the basic social revolutionary content of the movement is expressed. The national-liberationist idiom is, however, equally important when it represses and confines its social revolutionary content because that content can be accessed and foregrounded only when we recognise its repressed (absent or unconscious) presence in the conscious form. Such a constellational/'synchronic' conception, which is strictly theoretical and logical, should not be a pretext to paper over the empirical and formal historicity of various struggles, though. We cannot afford to conflate movements that are unconsciously social revolutionary with those that are self-consciously so. A constellational/'structural' view of history is merely meant to foreground the sedimented class reality of non-class, identitarian movements so that the fundamental impulse or aspiration of politics and movements can be underscored, if only to grasp their subsumption, distortion or betrayal. That is vital if the impulse is to be yet again foregrounded on the terrain of critical politics by setting the social revolutionary process free from its various *momentary* prisons. The essence must appear, not disguised as something else, but as its fully conscious self sans all mediatory distortions. It must, however, be borne in mind that the unconscious essence of politics can constitute itself only in relation to the conscious appearance of metapolitics. Its in-itself existence is notional, not real. For, the real is always defined and formed vis-à-vis the symbolic. The point then is that such appearance of the real as real can only be a provisional moment that indicates the actual non-alienated and dialectical logic of relationship between the two. Its critical revolutionary function, therefore, is to disabuse us of our understanding, till that moment, that the logic of this relationship is one of separateness, competition and domination.

It is this constellational formation of political resistance that compels Elias in *Sepai* to keep pulling the phenomenon of the Bangladeshi national-liberation struggle towards himself and pushing it away, obsessively doing both at one and the same instant. Such neurotic restlessness is not unusual. For what is constellational history if not an impossible representation of constant dialectical movement—of the singularity of a universal logic splitting into a plurality of particular forms, which once again dissolve into the singularity of the universal, which once again splits, *ad infinitum*. This is multiplicity, which presents differences (particular forms) as same (the singular logic embedded in them) even as it sees and shows the same (the singular logic) manifest by those differences. In such an order of things, the sameness of differences and the differences of the same appear all together and simultaneously.

Ghatak, in sharp contrast to Elias in *Sepai*, is not an obsessive 'multiplicist'. He is, much as he would want to be otherwise, a 'rejectionist' and 'chooser'. His politics and art, in the way they embody his concerns, seem to presume a world of heterogeneous forms that are all complete in themselves. Here *pre*-national 'organic' community is envisaged as a self-contained thing-in-itself, *prior* to and existentially independent of the nation-state. It is, therefore, seen to be completely *separate* from and *outside* the realm of alienating civil society of different individuals. Such a socio-political imagination compels Ghatak to view the preponderance of the nation-state as merely the result of competitive domination of the 'non-alienated' pre-capitalist communitarian *form* by the alienation-fostering bourgeois national *form*. *Jukti...*—which we analyse here because it is characteristically representative of Ghatak's political and aesthetic personality imbued as it is with the trauma of Partition—is an accurate expression of that imaginary. The film shows Neelkantha articulating his criticism of the Bangladeshi national-liberation war; not by engaging with it but by rejecting it for the lost idyll of an organic pre-national community.

For Ghatak, obtaining to an organic, non-alienated state of being is a matter of choosing one form of social organisation (pre-capitalist communitarianism) by rejecting another (the liberal nation of citizens), not of critical engagement with bourgeois nationhood, and its logic of alienation, to access the inverse logic of non-alienation immanent in them. So, while Elias sees in the national liberation project possibilities of a social revolution and their simultaneous cooption, for Ghatak all such possibilities exist outside and independent of this struggle, which for him is devoid of all revolutionary impulse. That is quite evident in Neelkantha's complete refusal to engage with the movement. He rejects the petty-bourgeois euphoria evoked by the liberation war in West Bengal. He presciently believes that the attendant nationalist fervour would, in the name of erasing religious differences to unite a divided Bengal, do no more than enable the petty-bourgeois elite from both sides to further close ranks against the subalterns.

Yet that belief is born, not through a process of critical engagement with the concrete conjunctural reality of national liberation, but from nostalgia for a non-alienated communitarian idyll that supposedly existed as a tangible material form prior to the advent of nationhood. Neelkantha does not even wish to account for how exactly the Bangladeshi national liberation struggle represses and betrays its social revolutionary impulse. For him a mere declaration of the problem would do. He is shown ranting against the "bourgeoisie" of two Bengals (Indian west and Pakistani/Bangladeshi east) for having lunged the "dagger" of national-liberationist betrayal into the back of the toiling masses. This illustrates quite well how Marxism can become an alibi for romantic communitarianism. And all of Ghatak's films, but particularly *Subarnarekha*, *Komal Gandhar* (*C-Minor*) and *Badi Theke Paliye* (*Escaping Home*), are replete with such examples.

The right statement made, the quest for possibilities of a non-alienated society unfolds—irrespective of the ongoing national liberation war—through a picaresque journey across the rural hinterland of Indian West Bengal. Neelkantha and his itinerant group of three encounter the possibilities of an organic Bengali community in folk art forms (Chau dance and its masks), tribal ways of life, demotic customs, and, last but not least, the unifying principle of the Mother cult and Naxal insurgency. All those experiences are significant in that they confront the modern and genteel linguistic-cultural Bengali 'nationhood' as its gothic, ugly, inchoate and self-destructive instincts, which it has purged itself of. The confrontation is staged to shock the 'nationalist' Bengali out of his culturally smug and complacent being and renew his ontological perception so that they are encountered, not as marginalised externalities of its social present, but as reminders of what Bengaliness was before its destructive and alienating national fate. The confrontation is, by that same turn of logic, equally an intimation of what Bengaliness can be once such a fate is shunned. Ghatak's approach, in his quest for a non-alienated world, is both a priori and transcendental. Pre-capitalist communitarianism is, for him, evidently both a prelapsarian world of organicity lost through the 'original sin' of nationalism, and the redemptive telos, which can be reached by subordinating the 'sinful' world of nationalism and nation-state to its divine dominion.

Yet, Ghatak's Neelkantha is unable to successfully reclaim that pre-national communitarian organicity, where Bengali 'genteelness' was integrated with and inflected by what it has expelled as common and vulgar in its 'period' of modern nationhood. He finds those common folks—his keepers of a happy and non-alienated communitarian conscience—driven by the alienating logic of competition and hierarchy in their struggle to preserve, ironically enough, their 'organic' identities. They are, therefore, condemned to conduct their struggle in terms of triumph or defeat for their identity. The stubborn refusal of a drunk Santhal, Neelkantha's violent fury notwithstanding, to admit that the local liquor they had been drinking was as much Bengali in provenance as Santhali bears that out.

Ghatak seems oblivious to the fact that the obverse of heterogeneity is homogenisation. While the former is the manifest reality, the latter is its impulse. In a world of heterogeneous forms, constituted by the logic of alienation and competition, the tendency of each of those forms is to always outcompete and dominate the rest in order to establish its homogenising hegemony. And that would be true in all cases, irrespective of whether one form dominates or the other.

The political struggle that Ghatak appears to conceive is merely about inverting the order of domination—pre-capitalist communitarianism over nationhood—not the erasure of the logic of competitive domination itself. The victory that such a struggle would yield is bound to be pyrrhic and a contradiction in terms. For, the moment the form of 'non-alienated' pre-capitalist community seeks to outcompete and dominate the form of bourgeois nationhood, it accepts its articulation by the logic of capitalist alienation. A pre-capitalist community does not defeat and displace nationhood; it becomes a nation itself.

Clearly, bourgeois nationhood and society have rendered the existence of organic and non-alienated communities *logically* impossible. And the only way to get around this impossibility is to self-consciously deploy the 'memories' of non-alienated pre-capitalism as a provisional ground, within the modern bourgeois social formation, for launching a critique of that logic of alienation. Pier Paolo Pasolini has deployed such politico-aesthetic tactics quite effectively in the films that comprise his *Trilogy of Life*. The cinematic adaptations of *The Decameron* (1971), *Canterbury Tales* (1972) and *Arabian Nights* (1974)—all carefully chosen mediaeval tracts of fables and parables on love and eroticism—are meant to be not so much depictions of communitarian manners of real love as an allusion through those depictions to the impossibility of love in an alienated and alienating capitalist society. Given that Italy of the early '70s was still largely in the cusp of transition from rural pre-modernity to modern urban-centric capitalism, the relevance of such tactics cannot be overstated.

But that was not Ghatak's way. His politics, dogged by the self-contradictions of its aprioristic/transcendental and parahistorical premises, left him with no choice but to fail, romanticise 'revolutionary' failure and unabashedly depict it. Such failure to reach the telos of an organic community arises from the impossibility of posing non-alienation as an end-in-itself. To envisage an end would be to signal the triumph of one moment over the rest. It would, by the same token, be an eternalised congealment of pure, unalienated and infinite becoming in that one moment. That would spell both alienation and competitive domination. Impossibility and failure on that score must, therefore, be read as alluding to the logical-critical functionality of 'pre-capitalist' communitarianism, vis-à-vis the logic of capitalist alienation. That, however, would be our "catastrophic" (Adorno; 2005, p. 42) reading of *Jukti*.... The film itself, thanks to its reification of failure, precludes such critical self-reflexivity. It is this self-consciousness that distinguishes Elias's politics and art from Ghatak's. The difference is most telling in the way they approach and deploy myths in their artistic creations. But to comprehend this difference, and particularly Elias's approach to myth, it is necessary that we unravel its politico-theoretical armature.

Historicising Myth : A Theoretical Detour

To appreciate the place of myths in Elias's politico-aesthetic paradigm, we need to understand the idea of myth as a kind of 'synchronic' or 'structural' history, which "has nothing to do with a present, eternal or otherwise, and is not to be grasped in terms of lived or existential time". (Jameson; 2007, p. 89.) This understanding would, among other things, also help us distinguish Elias's approach to myth and its 'pre-modern' order from that of Ghatak's. It would also serve to ground their respective political positions on nation, national-liberation and communitarianism—especially with regard to Partition of Bengal and the Bangladeshi national-liberation struggle—in the realm of theory.

In Elias, myth is imagined as a reality, which is absent in lived or existential time. The historiography, constitutive of such a vision, no longer envisages History as the unfolding of a narrative of occurrences in a temporal continuum. Instead, it renders History into a structure where everything is present all together: as much the manifest empirical reality of existence, as what this reality absents or represses and which therefore lies immanent in it. History becomes a kaleidoscope with all patterns inherent in it, even as the visibility (or not) of each of those patterns is contingent on how the kaleidoscope turns. It is like the (Japanese) fan of Benjamin's (1986, p. 6) memory, which keeps opening endlessly because no image can be entirely satisfactory as each image can be unfolded. For instance, here the historical image of existential reality can unfold into the image of what this reality has repressed, which in turn can once again unfold into its negative reality ad infinitum. Conversely, the fan in its folded moment holds all those infinite possibilities and is, therefore, simultaneously an expression of the image that is visible in its folded state and those that it can unfold into. In such circumstances, a myth can become its own critical-negative ground and, by extension, also that of the system that has constructed it as a myth. Myth can clearly cease to be myth. That should not, however, be confused with the affirmation of a myth's literal meaning.

To simply claim that a myth is true would be to accept the determinate mode—constitutive of existential time—that has designated it thus. Never mind that such designation is meant to denigrate its ontology as an impossible fable, and deny its epistemology as false. Such belief in the literalness of a myth would, then, be as much of a non-critical acceptance of existential time as when the truth and/or possibility of that myth is emphatically rejected. Clearly, all knowledge and experience in lived time, whether they exist in the form of dematerialised ideas or are instituted as sensory-empirical materiality, are theoretical objects of the prevailing determinate mode within which they have been produced.

Clearly then, critical-theoretical reality of a myth should not only be distinguished from its literal reality, it should be seen as inverting the latter's order in its entirety.

More accurately, reconstitution of myth as knowledge of its own theoretical-critical negativity should be seen as the production of a new theoretical object within a determinate mode that is different and discrete from the determinate mode that designates it as myth and is constitutive of our lived time.

To talk either of myths or the critical-theoretical knowledge immanent in them without first seeing them as specific theoretical objects constituted within their respective determinate modes would, if we were to follow in Balibar's (1999, p. 203) footsteps, be akin to Marx writing the first line of *The Communist Manifesto*—"The history of all hitherto existing society is the history of class struggle." It would, to paraphrase the French Marxist for our purposes, not be the first statement of our theory of the critical knowledge of myths, it would only "summarize the raw material of (our) work of transformation" of myths. The inspiration for this work of transformation can be drawn from Althusser and Balibar's (1997, p. 225) Marx for whom "the definition of every mode of production" is "a *combination* of (always the same) elements which are only notional elements unless they are put into relation with each other according to a determinate mode...". This also affords the possibility of "periodizing the modes of production according to a principle of *variation* of these combinations...".

And what are these different determinate modes if not various language-systems with their own singular rules of syntax and metaphor. Those different rules become manifest when apparently the same syntax, turn of phrase and/or vocabulary come to connote different orders of relationships among the same (notionally) constitutive elements in different discursive or determinate modes. And such discursive differences in connotation for what appears to be the same form of language must be ascribed to unique and singular sets of social practices that underpin and animate the language-form within their respective constitutive determinate modes. In short, each one of those language-systems (determinate modes) envisages a pattern of connections among elements unique and specific to it.

A myth should, then, be defined as a certain specific combination of notional elements, brought together in a certain relationship by the determinate mode of existential time. And its transformation into what can be defined as critical-theoretical knowledge can be understood, according to the principle of variation, as a change in connections and relations among the same elements within a different determinate mode. Balibar's (1997, p. 226) contention that Marx's analysis of a 'combination' (mode of production) was the analysis of "a system of 'synchronic' connexions obtained by variation" implies "the possibility of an *a priori* science of the modes of production, a science of *possible* modes of production, whose realization in real-concrete history would depend on the result of a throw of the dice or the action of an optimum principle". Considering that we are concerned here with understanding both myth and the critical real function it plays in Elias's novels, should we not extend the horizons of Balibar's "a priori science" to also include actual and possible modes of reality, knowledge and experience?

If myth is no more than a theoretical object produced within and by the determinate mode of bourgeois science, rationality and, most importantly, modern secular-democracy, it follows that outside such a mode its status as myth would be completely notional. It also follows, therefore, that within another determinate mode the connections among notional elements—which had in the preceding mode been constituted as myth—would get reorganised differently (according to the principle of variation) to produce a specific theoretical object which is assigned a different ontological-epistemological status of, say, non-myth. Once this theoretical possibility is established, the constitution, or signification, of the critical-negative ontology of myth as it were can be grasped better. The question now is, what would the motive force of this shift—from one determinate mode (of bourgeois rationality and secularism) to another (that of its critique)—be. Or, what impels the envisioning of this critical determinate mode? Unless that question is raised and an attempt is made to meaningfully answer it, we would remain blind, allegedly like Althusser and Althusserians, to the booby-trap of 'theoreticism'. Balibar's "throw of the dice or the action of an optimum principle" clearly needs to be grounded more rigorously.

Integral to such a line of inquiry is the question of agency. For, something has to impel someone. Put more simply, there has to be an agent, which is propelled by some force, to 'found' a determinate mode, in this case the critical determinate mode. Let us understand this interaction between the agent and its motive force more clearly. The agent in the process of embodying and practising the consciousness of myth, and all other forms of knowledge constituted by the established determinate mode, could come to a point where it realises that some or all forms of knowledge constituted by that mode militate against its 'true' self. This 'trueness' of self—which simultaneously and naturally 'falsifies' existential time, its realities and their determinate mode—is nothing but a function of resistance against the domination and determination of lived time. Clearly then, truths and falsehoods are no more and no less than representations of domination and struggle. Better still, they are conceptualisations of political practice of oppression and/or resistance. In a fundamental sense, therefore, all questions are questions of politics and power struggle, albeit disguised in the 'true-false' and/or 'right-wrong' idioms of knowledge and ethics respectively. Foucault—whose theory of discursive regimes of discourse has a strong methodological affinity with Althusser's philosophy of determinate modes—sought to indicate precisely this masking or articulation of power by knowledge and ethics when he self-reflexively proclaimed, "I have never written anything but fictions." This statement, contrary to what our postmodern friends might want to claim, is not a clarion call to political and ethical relativism. Why else would Foucault's intellectual peer, Deleuze (2007, p. 98), have responded thus: "But never has fiction produced such truth and reality."

Foucault's theory clearly needs to be grasped in all its complexity. His contention that "a statement has a 'discursive object' which does not derive in any sense from a particular state of things, but stems from the statement itself" (Deleuze; 2007, p. 8) does not imply that different knowledge-systems and experiences in lived time can have equal validity. Instead, he seems to suggest, through an implied dialectical logic, that an object of discourse, precisely because it has no reality outside the discursive field of that discourse, must have the freedom (power) to be reconstituted/resignified within a new discursive field as a completely different object with different meanings, uses and a new ontological reality.

Foucault's theory of discursive fields—if seen as a critical intervention in the domain of knowledge and its production at a concrete socio-historical moment—is a problematising rap on the knuckles of the modern Hegelian hierarchy of disciplines. In such a disciplinary scheme, a knowledge-system or discipline constitutes and defines itself only through a differential turn vis-à-vis all other disciplines, both lower and higher than it on the knowledge ladder. It is hardly surprising that such a situation should have institutionalised the violation of autonomous discursiveness of knowledge fields. This means that discourses do not appear as their own essence. Equally, objects of one discursive field have no power to move into another field, of which they can become the founding event even as they are reconstituted within it as new theoretical objects. In Foucauldian terms, the tendency of knowledge to become its own surface so that it can reside nowhere else but on it is curbed. Modern surfaces have, by becoming repressive lids, created their own depths which they then deign to express and distort.

Foucault's formulation is then a critique of an order of discourse integral to the capitalist political economy of exchange values, which engenders competition, alienation, hierarchy and dominance, and thus quells the constant becoming of an autonomous subject. His theory of discursive discourses must, in that context, be read as an ethics for a yet-to-emerge moment of socialised knowledge production, where the political economy of use value would come into its own. It would be a world, not of static and differential heterogeneities, but of dynamic and organic multiplicity.

This attempt to discover, or shall we say invent, a Marxian Foucault was doubtless a digression. But it is a productive one in that it enables us to foreground the essential relationship between knowledge/ethics and political power. In so doing we get the key to open the agency-motive force deadlock, vis-à-vis the emergence of a new determinate mode of critical knowledge. The political domination that individual/s from certain strata (or class) in an empirically existing social formation are likely to experience while embodying the knowledge-objects of its determinate mode can push them to resist such domination, and eventually the selfhood and knowledge that such domination imposes on them to strengthen its sway. Such resistance confers on them an evanescently autonomous subjectivity that impels them to imagine a new determinate mode of critical knowledge and being. This mode of reflection and practice rearranges the connections between the elements to simultaneously produce new theoretical objects, and a knowledge that can be said to be in concert with, indeed emerges organically from, their 'true' being. Even as it does that, the new mode breaks with the established determinate mode of existential time, which through and because of that break is critically designated as 'false'. But this account, its explanatory usefulness notwithstanding, is both mechanical and dialectically provisional. Worse, it does not pass muster with the Althusserian framework of structural causality. Such an explanation, whereby the emergence of a new determinate mode is made contingent on an autonomous agency completely precluded by the idea of determinate modes, becomes the *deus ex machina* of the Althusserian tangle. And it is condemned to play that role as long as Althusser's framework is not clarified in its conjunctural context.

Let us begin with Balibar's (1997, p. 252) tellingly limiting declaration on that score: "For each practice and for each transformation of that practice, they are the different forms of individuality which can be defined on the basis of its combination structure." His statement clearly precludes the possibility that a subject's revolutionary critical practice would induce it to imagine a new determinate mode of critical knowledge. For, the philosopher has subordinated subjectivity to the "combination structure" (or determinate mode) it was meant to found. Yet the problem remains: Althusser and Balibar's theory of combination structure does not ostensibly explain why or how a determinate mode of critical knowledge comes into being by breaking with the determinate mode of lived bourgeois knowledge. To say that revolutionary practice gives rise to the critical determinate mode that makes revolutionary practice possible amounts to no more than an absurdly un-self-conscious expression of the problem of infinite regress. That would, however, be an inevitable pitfall so long as problems of knowledge are posed only in conceptual terms. For, human language, in which all concepts are necessarily formulated, conceals metaphysics of linear temporality and causality. The problem can be overcome only if we see the two apparently irreconcilable and thus undialectical formulations of the relationship between structure (or theory) and agency (or practice)—where either structure can give rise to practice or practice can found structure—as conceptually frozen halves of a dynamic dialectical whole. That whole is more than the sum of its two halves as in motion each half is both itself and the other at the same time. Ilyenkov's (2008, p. 37) understanding of the abstract and the concrete, and the dialectic between them, could in this instance be illuminating.

"The concrete in thinking also appears, according to Marx's definition, in the form of combination (synthesis) of numerous

definitions. A logically coherent system of definitions is precisely that 'natural' form in which concrete truth is realised in thought. Each of the definitions forming part of the system naturally reflects only a part, a fragment, an element, an aspect of the concrete reality—and that is why it is abstract if taken by itself, separately from other definitions. In other words, the concrete is realised in thinking through the abstract through its own opposite, and is impossible without it. But that is, in general, the rule rather than an exception in dialectics. Necessity is in just the same kind of relation with chance essence with appearance, and so on."

To that list we ought to add 'theory with practice' and 'structure with agency'. We need to follow Ilyenkov (and Marx) to realise the concrete by thinking through the abstract of structure (or theory) through its own opposite of agency (or practice). The concrete, dialectical and dynamic whole would, in this case, be praxis, where its two fragments of theory and practice are themselves and each other simultaneously. It could be argued in a similar vein, that Althusser and Balibar's determinate mode of knowledge is both the product and producer of its own practice. And that this practice is as much its theoretical object as it is its singular founding event.

In any case, we should not overlook the fact that Balibar and Althusser's intervention was at an 'anthropomorphic' conjuncture within Marxist politics and theory. To that extent, their revolutionary intent to effectively confront the threat this conjuncture posed to Marxism in terms of evacuating it of all its historical materialist content and class struggle itself cannot surely be faulted. The anthropomorphism of a certain preponderant strain of "humanistic Marxism" had emphasised the problem of alienation of the individual by reifying and eternalising the historical individuality of bourgeois civil society and liberal-democracy. This amounted to wiping off, both deliberately and otherwise, the traces of historical production or constitution of individuality. Althusser and Balibar's response, not incorrectly, was to render the production of the Individual and various other historical individualities visible. And that led them to stress heavily, perhaps excessively, on the virtually de-emphasised objectivist aspect (determinate mode or combination structure) of Marxism. Their tactical attempt to give precedence to structural causality over practice and human subjectivity, if only to respond to the pressing revolutionary needs of their moment, did not blind them to the larger dialectical strategy, though. And that becomes evident when we contrast Althusser and Balibar's 'structuralism' with that of the structuralists.

In the latter, the basic units or elements (mytheme, phoneme, episteme, etc) are positive determinants of various combinatories. They have a meaning a priori to the various systems they constitute. In Althusser's 'structuralism', however, elements outside their determinate mode have merely a notional existence. They become real, or acquire any meaning, only in relation to each other in a determinate mode of knowledge, politics or practice. The privileging of connections between elements and their variations over the elements themselves, shows that Althusser's determinate mode is only a quasi-structure. Considering that relations, connections and their variations are, unlike the a priori elements of the structuralists, not conceptual fixities, it would be safe to claim that Althusser's structure formed and framed by such mobilities is no more than a conceptual-linguistic schema that mimics the dialectic of historical motion.

A couple of examples, which show how myths and 'true historical' knowledge can both be displaced from the determinate mode of instrumentalised bourgeois rationality into its critical mode where they are reconstituted as different theoretical objects, would be in order. Let's first train our sights on what is known as pre-capitalist communitarianism.

The determinate mode of existential time—which is the time of representative democracy, civil society, nation-states and capitalism—has constituted and signified 'pre-capitalism' as a thoroughly stratified and oppressive theoretical object. That does not, however, mean that this object, which can also be called 'pre-capitalist communitarianism' inhabits existential time only as a dematerialised idea. Its constitution as a stratified and oppressive object is also evident in sensory-empirical terms. The articulation of pre-capitalist communities within and by the determinate mode of capitalism is manifest in how various traditional, 'pre-capitalist' identities such as castes and religious communities have actually been put into relations of mutual hostility and domination by the logic of competition that arises from that determinate mode. In such circumstances, a critical determinate mode, constitutive of a possible time outside the one that we inhabit, can reconstitute pre-capitalism as a non-alienated and organic social formation. That is exactly what many of Pasolini's films, especially the ones cited earlier in this essay, do.

At the risk of doing some violence to our cardinal framework of determinate modes and theoretical objects, let us provisionally adopt the methods of empirical history to better understand the stratification-organicity binary in pre-capitalist communities. That would, if anything, only help us shore up the validity of our framework. Pre-capitalist communities have, in temporal-empirical history, been both stratified and organic. This strange paradox arises from the fact that while in economic terms those societies were stratified as surplus would be extracted by force, in psycho-cultural terms their ordinary denizens felt much less alienated than the average individual-citizen of modern civil society. After all, caste or religious community, which can be extremely coercive and totalitarian at functional level, also does give people even now a sense of familial closeness and social security. The competitive logic of capitalism has, in articulating the remnants of pre-capitalist communities, de-emphasised their psycho-cultural aspects even while accentuating their oppressive and hierarchical socio-economic dimensions.

Now for myth. Ernst Cassirer (1953, pp. 4-5), one of the key movers of the Neo-Kantian current in philosophy, employs the methods of comparative philology (or linguistics) to show how the Greek myth of Daphne and Apollo was, for the ancient Greeks, not a fictional myth at all but lived reality.

"Daphne, who is saved from Apollo's embraces by the fact that her mother, the Earth, transforms her into a laurel tree. ... it is only the history of language that can make this myth "comprehensible," and give it any sort of sense. Who was Daphne? In order to answer this question we must resort to etymology, that is to say we must investigate the history of the word. "Daphne" can be traced back to the Sanskrit Ahana, and Ahana means in Sanskrit the redness of dawn. As soon as we know this, the whole matter becomes clear. The story of Phoebus (Apollo) and Daphne is nothing but a description of what one may observe everyday: first, the appearance of the dawnlight in the eastern sky, then the rising of the sun-god who hastens after his bride, then the gradual fading of the red dawn at the touch of the fiery rays, and finally its death or disappearance in the bosom of Mother Earth. So the decisive condition for the development of the myth was not the natural phenomenon itself, but rather the circumstance that the Greek word for the laurel and the Sanskrit word for the dawn are related; this entails with a sort of logical necessity the identification of the beings they denote."

That an ancient Greek account of an observable natural phenomenon becomes for us, modern human beings, a myth is because the same set of linguistic statements are loaded with two completely different kinds of connotative charge within their respectively distinct discursive-linguistic modes. Cassirer (1953, p. 5) himself suggests as much when he approvingly quotes Max Mueller: "Mythology is inevitable, it is natural, it is an inherent necessity of language, if we recognize in language the outward form and manifestation of thought; it is in fact the dark shadow which language throws upon thought and which can never disappear till language becomes entirely commensurate with thought, which it never will." This implies, dialectically, that reality will always be apprehended through its symbolisation in language (discourse and/or practice) even as it will slip through its grasp like sand to necessitate its constant resignification. We can in terms of the discussion here, also take it to be an account of the perpetual shifting of determinate modes, which will constantly vary the pattern of relationship among their elements to resignify and reconstitute them as new objects.

Žižek (2003, p. 6) intends to emphasise precisely that when he summons Robert Pfaller's authority to argue that "the direct belief in a truth that is subjectively fully assumed ("Here I stand!") is a modern phenomenon, in contrast to traditional beliefs-through-distance, like politeness or rituals. Pre-modern societies did not believe directly, but through distance, and this explains, for instance, why Enlightenment critics misread "primitive" myths — they first took the notion that a tribe originated from a fish or a bird as a literal direct belief, then rejected it as stupid, "fetishist," naïve." But it is not Žižek's to merely prove how myths can be displaced from the determinate mode of bourgeois Enlightenment to be reconstituted as another possible existential reality. He is also implying the political necessity of that shift and displacement, if only to effect a critical resistance against the domination of the determinate mode of instrumentalised rationality and its constitutive bourgeois political economy.

The examples above indicate that there can be times and historical worlds, parallel to and outside the history of existential time, to which we, its inhabitants, can escape even as our ontologies are transfigured in the process. It is, however, equally evident that we can discern such possible realities—which are supposed to be constitutive of critical histories vis-à-vis the historical reality of existential time—only in their representations. We are constrained to access their possible *existence* only through the representational resources of language, discourse and practice available within lived time. Possible realities, as a result, come to inhabit the existential time of which they are presumed to be alternatives of. They thus end up articulating their logic of non-alienation and non-competition, paradoxically enough, through the theories, discourses and practices of alienation and competition constitutive of existential time. In such circumstances, we must learn to look *through* how they are being articulated (by the existential logic of alienation and competition) to *see* what they intend to articulate (the possible logic of non-alienation and non-competition).

All ideologies, including those that seek to critique the alienated/commodified reality (or ideology) of existential time of capitalism, are discernible only as commodities. Their representation within this time of capitalism, constituted by its regime of differential exchange values, renders them thus. This clearly means the relative importance of critical ideologies in capitalist society would be completely contingent on their valorisation through competition. In such circumstances, it would be unlikely that a critical ideology, which embodies the logic of non-alienation, would have many takers. The market would simply not ascribe as much value to an ideological commodity that threatens its survival, as it imputes to one (of alienation and competition) that constitutes and reinforces it.

And yet because the existential significance of such ideologies is contingent on the hope that they will overcome this logic of alienated and hierarchical valorisation, they need to create a demand for themselves. A demand that outstrips the demand for the alienating logic constitutive of lived time. This demand has to be for, not what the critical ideological commodity can immediately offer, but what it promises to deliver. It has to create a demand, not for possession but for hope. Hope, however, cannot in this instance be based on blind faith or superstition. It must produce proof. A critical ideology can deliver that proof by generating, what Alain Badiou (2006, p. x) terms, "reality effect" within existential time and its structure of reality. This effect of its non-alienated, non-competitive historical reality can be produced only if the ideology—irrespective of whether it is a conceptual/ aesthetic formulation or a mode of practice—self-reflexively includes within itself the historical location and process of its real emergence. It would, thereby, allude to the trans-representational, non-alienated logic implicit in it. A logic that effects complete and perfect consonance between essence and appearance, or reality and its representation. Such self-reflexivity, needless to say, would have to be a function of the style and/or technique of practice and/or conceptual formulation. The need for a 'theory of allusion to the implicit', to account for and measure the radical capacity of various seemingly disparate revolutionary practices and/or concepts, can hardly be overstated.

The Return: Ghatak's Failure And Elias's Deferred Success

It is on this terrain of reality effects and 'allusion to the implicit' that Elias's politico-aesthetic endeavour to reconstitute myths as critical-negative knowledge of our existential history must be comprehended and distinguished from Ghatak's 'mythic' vision of lived reality. Elias's narrative strategy or representational technique in *Khowabnama*, for instance, enables him to extract from certain traditional and syncretic folklore and fables of rural East Bengal the effect of a reality they critically and negatively posit. His use of the *khowab* (dream) trope to depict myths is meant to accomplish exactly that. He shows Tamijer Baap, a key character in the novel, encounter those fables in his dreams, thereby transforming those *fictions* into a reality of their own. After all, the dreamer experiences dreams as if they were real occurrences in a world he can only enter through sleep by leaving the world of wakeful, existential reality behind. There is then a world where dreams can cease being dreams to become reality. For, people know they had been dreaming only when the dream is over and they have woken up. The world of dreams, when a person is encountering it in his sleep, is absolutely real. It is, however, equally true that dream is not a thing-in-itself. Its existence, contingent on sleep, is bound to wakefulness in an inverse relationship. In short, dream and wakefulness are not separate realms-in-themselves, but are inflected by one another.

The reality-myth relationship, posed by Elias as one between wakefulness and dream, is rendered through this dialectic into a relationship between two realities—one existential while the other absent but possible. It also means that existential reality can travel down the strand of its inverse relationship with dream—which is simultaneously rendered into yet another, possible reality—to *become* that. The distinction between 'myth' (as fiction or transcendental faith) and 'reality' (as existential fact) is, as a result, obliterated. Such obliteration is for, example, evident in the way the ghost of a local Muslim ascetic—apparently killed in the anti-British Fakir-Sanyasi rebellions of late 18th-early 19th century—and other associated fabulistic events keep irrupting into and transfiguring the existential reality of Tamijer Baap in his sleepwalking reveries and activities. Those fables are, in the process, transformed from being fantastic, awe- and faith-inspiring tales into stirring memories of glorious resistance against oppression. Needless to say, the extractive oppression of the British East India Company of 18th-19th century and the exploitative ways of the local landlords and rich peasants of the 1940s are, their separation in time notwithstanding, integrated into the same historical-logical constellation. It's, however, through mendicant Cherag Ali, Tamijer Baap's spiritual mentor, that Elias is able to establish this logic of dissolution on firmer foundations. A dream-reader, Cherag Ali interprets dreams through the prism of doggerels and limericks of his mystic tradition as intimations of things to come in the existential-temporal continuum. His reading of dreams grounds them—together with the incantatory magic of his "authorless", mystic rhymes—in lived reality. Once again dreams and fables, thanks to such interpretation, are deemed real possibilities. They lose their mysterious depths, because of this interpretative turn, to become their own *real*, comprehensible surfaces.

What changes, therefore, are not merely the ontologies of myth and existential reality but, more importantly, the relationship between the two. In fact, the two different ontological situations—of myth-reality on one hand, and possible reality-existential reality on the other—are functions of two different orders of relationship. In the first case, it's a relationship of alienation, domination and one-way determination. Existential reality dominates over myth (or dream), as if the latter were a realm separate from and outside it, and determines its meaning by denying it the possibility of expressing any reality other than the one it has been framed in. In the second instance, the relationship is between two different moments of the same process. Here, lived reality and what it has designated as myth are not separate from each other but are like two points in a flowing stream. Different points that flow into each other to become one.

Ghatak's idea that lived reality conceals mythic substructures, which determine it, is in sharp contrast to this dialectical-logical approach towards myths. If we were to follow Ghatak's aesthetic-philosophical logic and realise, not merely in ideas but in our existence, the mythic archetype of our lived reality, it would mean that myths become existential reality. But do we then stop there as if the hidden truth of our existence has become apparent and our 'true' selves have, in the process, been rendered free? The answer, as far as Ghatak is concerned, is a resounding yes. In *Meghe Dhaka Tara* (Cloud-capped Star), the crushed and exploited existence of protagonist Nita, a typical representative of Bengali womanhood, is sought to be shown and explained fully in terms of the figure of Mother goddess, a mythic image of the self-sacrificing provider in Bengali culture and imagination. Someone could, of course, claim through a dialectical reading of the film that Ghatak has historicised the myth of the Mother Goddess in terms of the exploitative reality of the post-Partition refugee Bengali woman. And that would, without doubt, be an honourable revolutionary intention to ascribe to the text of the film. It is, however, equally our task to know whether, and how far, does this intention of the text coincide with the intention of the author.

The absolute pessimism in which the filmmaker steeps the possibility of Nita's emancipation, by evoking a melodramatic ambience of despair towards the end of the film, clearly suggests that there is no escape for her from her myth-ordained fate. It, therefore, also shows that for Ghatak, the historicisation of lived reality is merely its reduction to a mythic archetype. The filmmaker's aesthetic imaginary anticipates, arguably, his impossible, failure-ridden political project of establishing the domination of 'organic' communitarianism over alienating nationhood, paradoxically to end the domination and exploitation of modern bourgeois nations. Even revolution becomes, in *Nagarik* (Citizen), a matter of fate. The film, true to Ghatak's philosophical-aesthetic programme of unearthing mythic sub-structures of lived reality, appears to suggest that the exploitation, progressive immiseration of the refugees from East Bengal, and the consequent socio-political unrest on the streets of Calcutta, is no more than the playing out of the mythic *yuga*ic cycle.

Ghatak's (2000, p. 36) mythic a prioriism is starkly evident in this theorisation of his cinematic aesthetics:

"Since Depth Psychology and Comparative Mythology have laid bare certain fundamental workings of the human psyche as ever recurring constellations of primordial archetypes, our task today has become easier.

We now know, all that creates art in the human psyche also creates religion; a medicine man, a 'shaman', a 'rishi' a 'poet', and a 'village woman possessed by seizure' are, fundamentally, set in motion by the same or similar kinds of unconscious forces.

And these forces are the very ones which are continually nourishing the subjective psychic bond, giving an inner subjective correspondence to the objective creation around us.

It follows that all art is subjective. Any work of art is the artist's subjective approximation of the reality around him. It is a sort of reaction set in motion by the creative impulse of the human unconscious."

This theorisation is complete if it is seen merely as an attempt by an artist to explain his art as an expression of his moment. But read as a politico-aesthetic programme it is, at best, partial and at worst, undialectically mysterian. None can dispute the fact that "any work of art is the artist's subjective approximation of the reality around him". Yet, that statement can sum up a revolutionary philosophical aesthetic programme in its completeness only if it manages to yet again collapse that subjectivity into its constitutive objective reality and, most importantly, its political praxis. In Ghatak's (2000, p. 37) imagination, "dialectics is *born*: the interplay of the subjective and the objective" "in the objectivisation of this essentially subjective element". (Emphasis mine.)

This understanding of dialectics as merely the primacy of subjective over objective robs it of its processual logic by rendering it into a phenomenon and an ontology: an eternalised closure of the process of infinite becoming in one of its moments. That amounts to the un-self-conscious triumph of phenomenology and its logic of alienation over the idea of subtracted ontology and its logic of pure becoming. Ghatak's art, and his aesthetic programme, do not radiate self-awareness. They do not seem to express the idea that mythic sub-structures of lived historical time are useful only to the extent that they indicate, through their negative-critical and possible reality, the transformation of the logic of alienation, opposition and oppression into an unalienated logic of horizontal process.

Myth, as Elias has shown, can seek to free itself of its falsified ontology, imposed on it by the repressive workings of existential reality, not by being existential reality, but by allusively critiquing the logic of alienation that is constitutive of beings and the idea of ontology. The critical power of myths, vis-à-vis existential reality, lies not so much in their having become empirical reality of existence from the absent negative reality they were, but in the logic of processual becoming that this transformation alludes to.

This lack of self-awareness and self-reflexivity in Ghatak's cinema and his politics could be located in his theoretical dependence on psychologist Carl Jung's idea of the collective unconscious. For Jung, unlike Freud, the unconscious is not existentially constituted by the conscious mind and in inverse relation to it; it is a kind of a collection of man's animal instincts that exists as a thing-in-itself and prior to the advent of the consciousness of rational human being. The unconscious in Jung is a misnomer. To call it pre-conscious would actually make it more theoretically consistent.

But it is not as if the awareness of a non-alienated relational logic between myth and existential reality as two moments of the same process of constant becoming is discernible in Elias's novel (*Khowabnama*) as the self-consciousness of characters who embody it. The sleepwalking reveries of Tamijer Baap, or the Delphic reading of dreams by Cherag Ali are, without doubt, moments when myths irrupt into lived history obliterating themselves and that history in the process. But those moments, considering that they happen to them as individuals, do no more than allude to the possibility of such obliteration for their entire community. The two personas in question are characterologically constrained to merely experience that possibility as individuals, not access and foreground the revolutionary transformative impulse that resides in the sediments of their ecstasy and intoxication. Those characters and their 'obliterative' aptitudes are, as a result, condemned to be included on the margins of oppressive existential time as suspect, despicable, frightening, irrational and even false. Such differential inclusion also involves repression of the possible realities their aptitudes and personas posit and, as a consequence, pre-empts all efforts towards the collective realisation of those possibilities. Those characters, notwithstanding the critical-obliterative potential inherent in their mystic-hallucinatory energies of intoxication, are condemned to be oppressed and dominated by the lived time of rich peasants such as Sharafat Mandal and the power-hungry and effete politicians of the Muslim League and the undivided Communist Party of India respectively. This is in large measure due to their historical lack of awareness about the revolutionary potential of their aptitude for 'intoxication', which by itself is never good enough. For, as Benjamin (1986, p. 190) says, "...to place the accent exclusively on it would be to subordinate the methodical and disciplinary preparation for revolution entirely to a praxis oscillating between fitness exercises and celebration in advance. Added to this is an inadequate, undialectical conception of the nature of intoxication.... Any serious exploration of occult, surrealistic, phantasmagoric gifts and phenomena presupposes a dialectical intertwinement to which a romantic turn of mind is impervious. For histrionic or fanatical stress on the mysterious side of the mysterious takes us no further; we penetrate the mystery only to the degree that we recognize it in the everyday world, by virtue of a dialectical optic that perceives the everyday as impenetrable, the impenetrable as everyday."

The knowledge of a non-alienated, dialectical relationship between myth and existential reality is, therefore, expressed in the novel through the narrativising voice of its author. This authorial voice does not, however, come across as an expression a priori to and independent of the happenings in the novel. It is, instead, their constitutive narrative glue. Elias's representational strategy, which depicts myth as dream to indicate the non-alienated relationship between existential reality and myth, emanates from his politics of engaging with existential time without either fully embracing or rejecting it. To that extent, his determinate/discursive mode, within which the discourse of myth is reordered, and articulated as a critique of the alienating logic of existential time, is constituted by the author's affirmative identification with the militant praxis of classical revolutionary politics. And to this Elias alludes, self-reflexively, through the character of Keramat Ali, a poor peasant who attempts to takes mystic Cherag Ali's poetic tradition forward. Keramat, purportedly inspired by Cherag Ali, becomes a wandering minstrel in a Tebhaga-struck swathe of East Bengal. There is, however, one very crucial difference between the "student" and his "master". The former does not, like the latter, recite poetry bestowed on him by a depersonalised mystic and mythic tradition. He is a singer of new, self-composed songs whose authorship he unabashedly claims. His songs are obviously not interpretations of dreams and myths. They are an expression of his community's new existential reality: the uprising of poor sharecroppers and landless labourers against an exploitative and oppressive landed gentry, and subsequently the Muslim League's demand for an "egalitarian" Pakistan. Keramat's continuity and break with Cherag Ali, at one and the same time, portrays the transformation of the mystic-mendicant historical individuality of Cherag Ali into a different historical individuality, that of a revolutionary poet. The latter is both a doer (militant) and a thinker (poet), and is thus part and parcel of a praxis, which engenders the reality and logic of pure, unalienated becoming against the dominant existential reality of alienation and exploitation. This praxis, and the militant/poetic historical individuality constitutive of its revolutionary mode, is born out of a community's urge to emancipate itself from oppression and render its repressed ontology and epistemology valid. It is, simultaneously, the event that triggers the awareness of such oppression and alienation. Here we have a tangible example of something we dealt with in the abstract earlier: the dialectic of how a new determinate mode is founded by an evental/revolutionary subject, which is simultaneously constituted as an individuality of this revolutionary mode of doing and reflection. But what is perhaps most important is that the two characters of Cherag Ali and Keramat Ali, united by a troubadour's tradition but separated by the break that Keramat has introduced into it, constitute a narrative device that Elias employs to show how an oppressed and exploited individual, when he becomes a militant against such depredations, breaks with existential history to inhabit a different historical reality and time. The determinate mode constitutive of this new reality and time puts him (an element) in a new relationship with all others (remaining elements) of his society and, in the process, assigns him with a new ontological self. Militant-poet Keramat Ali is, therefore, none other than Late Cherag Ali, who has broken with his earlier mystic-mendicant self to become a revolutionary bard. And this break happens because Cherag Ali's dream-reading vocation had transformed him into an inflection point between existential reality and its critical-negative knowledge in myths. Thus mystic poet Cherag Ali has, in the process of becoming militant poet Keramat, merely turned his face away from the oppressive reality of existential wakefulness to travel down the strand of inverse relationship that links this wakefulness to mythic mystic dreams, if only to realise in empirical-material terms the critique of the alienating logic of existential time that those myths had negatively posed in his 'mystic' interpretations.

The Althusserian homology of the break between Early Cherag Ali and Late Cherag Ali a la Keramat, can be extended to show that Elias—whose *Khowabnama* posits a new determinate mode within which myths are reconstituted as critical-negative knowledge of the existential reality of 1940s' Bengal—is none other than Late Keramat Ali. He could perhaps, by that same logic, also be called Very Late Cherag Ali. *Khowabnama*'s critical determinate mode is not possible without the revolutionary praxis of Tebhaga, whose legacy Elias inherited. It is only in and through its evental praxis—which presented a lived, material, empirical critique and alternative to the alienating and exploitative logic of 1940s' Bengal—that mythic 'fictions' could be re-imagined as realities repressed by an oppressive and alienating existential reality. They could, therefore, also be posed as the negative-critical knowledge of such reality. There is, however, a problem. A struggle like Tebhaga is bound to be articulated by the existential-historical logic of alienation, competition and domination. The oppositional stance of all such struggles, with regard to oppression and/or exploitation indicates that. We, who live and do politics in the shadow of Soviet collapse and the Chinese perversion, should always remember that such oppositional struggles are not meant to end in the *domination* of labour over capital.

Labour does not dominate capital it becomes capital itself. Such working class movements, in spite of being posed and articulated in oppositional terms, must exude the awareness that they are part of a larger continuous struggle that constantly seeks to decimate both capitalism and the ontology of 'working people' within it. The struggle is actually about obliterating the difference between dominator and dominated, not the triumph of the latter over the former. Elias alludes to that implicit logic of revolutionary politics through *Khowabnama* when he depicts myths as dreams.

Tamijer Baap and Cherag Ali, by virtue of being members of the poor rural underclass of 1940s' East Bengal, are compelled to confront the oppressive existential reality with their 'dreamy' myths of rebellion and emancipation. Yet, in being posed as dreams, myths become as much a negation of the alienating logic of existential reality as the confrontational stance that such logic compels them to strike against that reality. In Elias, myths and their oppressed bearers confront existential reality and its oppressive purveyors not to defeat or dominate them, but to dissolve the boundaries that separate them and in the process transfigure their own existential ontology. Myth and reality, in his scheme, are related to each other, not through what appears to be the logic of absolute separation and opposition, but through a logic of inflection and perpetual process.

Such a historical relationship can, as we have seen above, also be conceived and represented as a 'synchronic' constellation of existential and possible (mythic) realities. Elias's 'structural' constellation of realities has the oppressive pre-Tebhaga existential reality of 1940s' East Bengal 'synchronically' integrated with the equally lived reality of the Tebhaga movement through a relationship of resistance against the former's logic of alienation and exploitation. The Tebhaga movement, in turn, is bound by the logic of anti-exploitative struggle with the 18th-19th century Sanyasi and Fakir rebellions, which in turn inflect the oppressive pre-Tebhaga existential reality as its inverted-critical knowledge in the form of myths. Those myths, especially in the critique they negatively pose to the alienating and exploitative logic of pre-Tebhaga Bengal, are integrated with the Tebhaga struggle as an alternative possible reality that the struggle seeks to accomplish. Elias constructs this kaleidoscopic world of infinite historical inflections in *Khowabnama* to allude to the possibility that this *fiction* on Tebhaga within his, and subsequently our, existential time of alienation is seen inflecting that lived reality as its critical-negative possibility. The fabulistic texture that Elias gives to slain militant Tamij, who with his bullet-riddled neck climbs into the moon, echoes the local myth of the dead Muslim ascetic, who after he had been killed by the East India Company had made his home on a local tree. His deliberate mythification of the reality of Tebhaga as depicted in his novel is supposed to negatively imply the possible reality of his *fiction* and thus open, not close, the dialectic. It is a possibility that waits to be actualised through collective political action. Much like Keramat and Tamij's rebellion actualised the reality immanent in the fables and dreams of their oppressed community.

Ghatak sees a beginning that has been lost and an end that cannot be reached. So, there is failure. For Elias, however, there is neither beginning nor end. There is only a never-ending journey with halting stations along the way. Success exists only in deferment and failure there is none. There is, however, a problem: we stop at one of those halting stations for far too long.

Note: The germ of the idea that is this essay is the result of a critical engagement with 'History's Creative Counterpart', a paper on Akhtaruzzaman Elias by critic Shubhoranjan Dasgupta.

BIBLIOGRAPHY

Adorno, Theodor W., *Aesthetic Theory*, tr. Robert Hullot-Kentor (Viva-Continuum, London, 2005)

Badiou, Alain, *Metapolitics* (from Jason Barker's introduction to it), tr. Jason Barker (Verso, London, 2006)

Balibar, Étiene, 'The Basic Concepts of Historical Materialism'. In *Reading Capital* by Louis Althusser and Etienne Balibar, tr. Ben Brewster (Verso, London, 1999)

Balibar, Étiene, 'The Elements of the Structure and their History'. In *Reading Capital* by Louis Althusser and Etienne Balibar, tr. Ben Brewster (Verso, London, 1999)

Benjamin, Walter, 'A Berlin Chronicle'. In *Reflections*, tr. Edmund Jephcott (Schocken Books, New York, 1986)

Benjamin, Walter, 'Surrealism'. In *Reflections*, tr. Edmund Jephcott (Schocken Books, New York, 1986)

Cassirer, Ernst, *Language and Myth*, tr. Susanne K. Langer (Dover Publications, New York, 1953)

Deleuze, Giles, *Foucault*, tr. Sean Hand (Viva-Continuum, London, 2007)

Ghatak, Ritwik, 'Cinema and the Subjective Factor'. In *Rows and Rows of Fences* (Seagull Books, Calcutta, 2000)

Elias, Akhtaruzzaman, *Chilekotar Sepai* (The University Press Limited, Dhaka, 2000)

Elias, Akhtaruzzaman, *Khowabnama* (Naya Udyog, Kolkata)

Ilyenkov, Evald V., *The Dialectics of the Abstract and the Concrete in Marx's Capital*, tr. Sergei Syrovatkin (Aakar Books, New Delhi, 2008)

Jameson, Fredric, *Archaeologies of the Future* (Verso, London, 2007)

Žižek, Slavoj, *The Puppet And The Dwarf* (The MIT Press, Cambridge, Massachusetts, 2003)

6

Kafka and the Question of Revolutionary Subjectivity

I

To talk about Kafka is to talk of the law and its exception by other means. Exception is created within and by the law to make the latter possible. Like bare life is produced by the law to protect high life on whose behalf it speaks. So, exception is included by excluding. And through its inclusion into law, by it being named as bare life by that law, it is excluded from it. Exception not only proves the law, it is also constituted by it. Clearly, the search by the exception for emancipation from the law, even as it maintains its ontology as 'exception', is impossible. Since this exception constitutes the law, its existence reinforces the law and will thus not permit liberation for its ontic position from the law, which can only happen through their mutual abolition. It only (pseudo-) liberates the holders of the exception position at one moment, only by pushing them on to the ontic position of the apparent subject of the law. Josef K's constant failure in *The Trial* to figure out his crime though his absurd encounters within the domain of the law shows how crimes are constituted by law in order for it to make and sustain itself.

II

In Kafka's 'Before the Law', the man from the country is prevented by the doorkeeper of the door of the law to open the shut door to discover the meaning of the law that lies beyond it. He wants to cross the threshold of the law to find out what comes before or prior to the law, which determines his place in the universe of his existence by giving him his being and its meaning within it. He–that law-determined being manifest in the case of this parable as the "man from the country"–wants to know what the law is (means) and how does it become possible and come to be. What, kind of, necessitated it. (The emphasis on the word 'know' above will become progressively clear as we go ahead with our analysis. For now, it would suffice to stick with the plot of the tale.) The man waits and spends his entire lifetime before that shut door, trying to persuade the doorkeeper, without success, to allow him through it. At the end of his life the doorkeeper tells the man from the country that the door was meant for him but he had not tried hard enough to pass through it. The ironical, almost paradoxical, and seemingly absurd note on which Kafka ends this fable is meant to indicate the impossibility for a being, whose very existence is made possible by the law insofar as the latter creates it, to go outside and beyond the law to discover what lies prior to it. For, a being created by the law cannot step outside of it without obliterating and erasing itself. And if and when such erasure of the being happens, it obviously cannot know what lies outside or prior to the law. In that sense, the door of the law, in 'Before the Law', cannot be opened to the outside because there is no outside to the law. The door, even if the doorkeeper had not been around, would have opened out into nothing—no-outside. In fact, they would have opened out into the law itself. That is, clearly, because the outside of the law—the outlaw—is already within it by being its outside. In other words, the outlaw (exception) is constitutive of the law. Law makes itself happen by defining itself with regard to something that is defined in the same movement as-not-the-law, as outside it. The law creates its own outside in order to make itself existentially possible. The law creates its outside even as this outside simultaneously creates the law. The dialectic in this is that the law includes by excluding and excludes by including. The modern capitalist order, in which people, ideas, things and so on are at once hierarchically excluded and productively included is a concrete manifestation of this abstract dialectic of the law.

The law, Kafka shows us by attempting to reduce it to its zero-point, has no meaning outside its fact of being a pure force of domination and determination. Its only meaning is just that. In politics, this problem is captured in sovereignty struggles and rights-based movements where the oppressed of a temporal moment might escape their oppression at another temporal moment but oppression per se does not disappear. If anything, the oppressed keep escaping their oppression by turning oppressors. Thus the diachronicity—or historical change—that such struggles evidently and consciously articulate is apparent and even false as they are caught in the same synchronic vector (history). Such diachronicity is, to my mind, merely temporal and not historical because a real (historical) diachronicity—as opposed to simple quantitative flow of time that according to me characterises temporal diachronicity–founds a new movement or flow of time in a qualitatively different historical direction than what precedes it. Time by itself is—following Walter Benjamin who said that time can be counted but not numbered—merely scalar. It is history and historical ruptures that transform it into a vector with direction whereby the counting of time also becomes its numbering.

III

Integral to this vision of the law in Kafka is the impossibility of knowing or being a being that can reach a goal. K's interminable approaching of the castle is a case in point. The more he tries to get there the more his motion seems to regress. It is as if he is merely going through the motions of walking forward (towards the castle), by standing at one point, without actually doing so. The knowing process or subject that originates that process constitutes the object of knowing, as something outside of the knowing subject that has to be known by that subject. For, knowing will not be possible if it does not have an outside that can be known. By the same token, this object in its condition of existence outside the knowing subject, which is of course designated thus by that subject, constitutes the knowing act. Thus the real concrete nature of something cannot be 'known' as it is constituted by the knowing process and the knowing subject, whose identity, by virtue of being made possible by the 'on-the-outside' existential condition of the 'object-to-be-known', cannot in turn be ascertained independent of the act of knowing at a certain moment. Knowing the concrete will, paradoxically, always yield abstractions.

It is this antinomy of knowing that Kant sought to overcome by introducing the ahistorical phenomenon-noumenon distinction and the a priori rationality of the knowing subject. Kafka brings this repressed antinomy to the fore by alluding to the despair occasioned by the constant and continuous slipping away of the concrete/real in the form of the castle or the applause for the hungry artist the more they are sought after (by K and the Artist in *The Castle* and 'The Hungry Artist' respectively) to be known. Ultimate applause will be heaped on the hungry artist only after he has starved himself to death. But then he will not receive any of that applause because he wouldn't any longer be there. Kafka hinted at this impossibility—which sharpens the modern finite human being's ever-insatiable desire to overcome the impossibility into a fruitless obsession that he cannot rid himself of, thereby making the impossibility progressively keener—when he wondered in a diary entry whether the shoes and clothes in his closet were the same when he was not looking at them.

IV

The sharply despairing apprehension of, nay confrontation with, such antinomies and paradoxes in Kafka ought to be ascribed to his Hasidic sensibility and its preoccupation with the idea of the invisible Jew. A preoccupation that has predisposed the Jews to believe the coming of the messiah is perpetually deferred.

The striving for the messiah that such sensibility and belief produces is, not surprisingly, always articulated as not yet, thereby tendentially implying that the messiah will come here within our given universe of the law where it cannot come yet, thanks to the counter-tendency inherent in this same striving. Clearly, the law cannot give way to the messianic unless the exception—the not-yet-but-yet-to-come of the messiah—which is constitutive of the law, is abolished thus also abolishing the law. The Pauline Christ-event of the moment of Christianity's birth in and through Saint Paul's epistolary interventions inaugurates—as shown by Alain Badiou and propagated by Slavoj Žižek—precisely such a new diachronic moment and movement. A moment of the actual arrival of the messiah in the shape of Jesus crucified and resurrected that is constitutive of a subtracted 'lawless' space outside and beyond the law and knowledge (as wisdom or doxa) , where it is not as if one doesn't know or is being lawless but where one does not need to know or be subordinated to the law. That is because matter is, in such a situation, its own subjectivity, which otherwise would be open to be known by a subject from its outside.

As for law, the existence of the subject in its singularity is its universal truth. Thus universality, in such a condition, is the auto-referentiality of the singular subject, which does not need to be designated and named as an ontology from a universalising outside termed the law. Clearly then, the condition of the subject's singular existence is its law, which is negation of negation as a law that does not determine or designate the subject from the latter's outside is an inversion of the logic of law and is thus not law at all. In the same vein, the subject is not a subject as it is not designated, determined and produced by law from its outside. Or, to be more accurate, it is named and produced by law that is not law. Since the subject is its own law, and the law its own object, what is named as the subject is only a provisional political naming of the trans-subjective at its one particular moment where it constitutes and expresses itself.

The law is constitutive of a condition that renders singular existence impossible by splitting the trans-subjective (or pure becoming), or the subject that expresses the trans-subjective at one finite moment of its many moments that constitute its infinity, into subject-object or universal-particular; or into heterogeneous strata of broken moments. In the Christ-event of Pauline Christianity, the messiah by actually arriving, abolishes the exception constitutive of the law and thus abolishes the law and its logic too. This is the path of, dare I say, anti-Judaic revolutionary politics, which produces a disjunction in the universe and discourse of the law to shift the ground of existence on to a space that is the logical inverse of the paradigm of law and law-produced being.

It is this that is missing in Kafka's consciousness, thanks to it being grounded in the Jewish-Hasidic sensibility. And it is this Hasidism that is at the root of Kafka's despairing optimism when he tells Max Brod that there is infinite hope "but it's not for us (humans)". This Jewish pessimism of Kafka articulates a tripartite schema wherein man is in between three conditions of being: the life of a burden of the law, which he is condemned to impossibly strive to be redeemed of; death that will extinguish the being that needs to be redeemed, rendering the question of redemption irrelevant; and, therefore, infinite hope outside of this life-and-death binary of a law-designated being. Such hope is vested in the figure of the messiah, whose arrival is always expected but perpetually deferred. This peculiar nature of the Jewish messiah, clearly, renders it into the negative exception to the given universe of the law—constituting it by making it possible and sustaining it.

Immanent in Kafka's Jewish pessimism about the fate of 'human beings' is, however, the realisable possibility of a trans-human and trans-being existence. This immanent unconscious of Kafka's Jewish consciousness, implicitly articulated by the tripartite schema we have extracted from him, is allegorically expressed by the actual coming of the messiah in Jesus, resulting in the rupture-like birth of Christianity from Judaism. The actual arrival of the messiah, as we have seen above, abolishes the exception of the yet-to-come-but-ever-not-here messiah and thus also ends up abolishing the given universe of the law and the existential condition of the law-designated, law-governed being. As a result, it also renders the fact of death of such a being into a redundant and meaningless idea. For, if within this horizon of non- or post-law the existence of being is not possible—because the pre-condition of being's existence is the law—there can be no question of his death! The condition of life within this new horizon is the trans-human or trans-being condition. Christ's second life, after he rises from the dead, is a metaphor of precisely such a trans-human life where the question of human death has been abolished, and rendered pointless and absurd.

This 'Christian' horizon is the horizon of Marxist revolutionary politics where one does not constantly and impossibly seek the yet-to-come-but-ever-not-here messiah, but where one is permanently restoring to the Church and its laws their originary and constitutive message and logic of messianic grace by, ironically enough, repeatedly decimating the churches and its laws. The death of a church of one moment is, within this horizon, not to be construed as the death of a being because what is preserved is the pure becoming or trans-subjectivity that formed that church but was also repressed by its reified institutionality. So, the death of a church (institution) of a moment, within this horizon, is the continuation of the trans-subjective life that was expressed in and by that church at that moment; but in so doing it also began threatening that life and therefore had to be destroyed to preserve the becoming-life that was constitutive of its existence. Within this horizon what lives is trans-subjectivity and the death of its one subjective expression of one particular moment is not a death because what lives through and in this apparent death, and matters, is the trans-subjectivity that also, dialectically speaking, lived in the coming-to-life of that church.

It is this immanence in Kafka's riddles of the law and its exception, and the possibility that this immanence can be actualised, that drew the Marxist in Benjamin to the Czech-German writer. To that extent, Benjamin's notion of Kafka, and his concomitant understanding of the writer's work, was very different from the sense imputed to him by vulgar Communist Party-type Marxists and, ironically, even the anti-communist dissidents, who pride themselves as being votaries of a politics of high culture free from the exigencies and vagaries of politics proper. Both cherish Kafka for what they see as his depiction of the hapless everyman face-to-face with a bureaucratic and totalitarian behemoth. That can and must, of course, be read into Kafka. But such a reading would do justice to both Kafka's aesthetic complexity and to a nuanced and effective counter-hegemonic politics only if the horror of bureaucratisation and totalitarianism are discerned in his work as a derivative and supplementary epiphenomenon of and within the essentially constitutive field of the law.

V

In that context, the case of Milan Kundera, especially his reading of Kafka, is a curious expression of the problem. Kundera, commenting on Kafka (and Jaroslav Hašek, Hermann Broch and Robert Musil), writes: "...it would be wrong to read their novels as social and political prophecies, as if they were anticipations of George Orwell! What Orwell tells us could have been said just as well (or even much better) in an essay or pamphlet." Kundera is right when he argues Kafka ought not to be conflated with Orwell. His criticism of those Kafka scholars, who read in the Czech-German writer the description of man's encounter with bureaucracy and totalitarianism, is entirely valid. And yet, Kundera's reading into Kafka of the bureaucratisation and totalisation of every sector, nook, cranny and crevice of modern human society—indeed, the very soul of the human being—takes us only one step away from the descriptions of the manifest forms, artifacts and apparatuses of bureaucratisation that are constitutive of and central to the Orwellian reading of Kafka that Kundera rejects.

Instead of describing the congealed forms of bureaucratisation, Kundera finds in Kafka the situations that put those forms in a certain relation to one another. That is, at best, a more refined version of Albert Camus' existentialist appropriation of Kafka. Kundera, thanks to his 'situationist' reading of Kafka, remains distant from Kafka's central concern, which, to my mind, was to articulate the essential logic that constituted and was constituted by bureaucratic and totalitarian situations. In Kafka, situations are merely incidental epiphenomena of the essential logic. They thwart Kafka's endeavour to efface himself so that language can emanate on its own from the non-lingual and the non-formal. In short, from the essence.

Kafka, the writer, is condemned to use language and thought to undermine language and thought themselves by attempting to capture the flux of the dialectical essence that lurks ghost-like in the depths of forms and concepts made possible by language. It is, as if, Kafka constantly conspires to set up a traumatic encounter of the symbolic (linguistic/conceptual/formal/situational) with the real, which is nothing but a trans-conceptual and/or formless dialectical logic constitutive of bureaucratic situations and orders. That is made manifest by the 'unreal' economy and sparseness of style in Kafka's writing. This then is the impulse behind Kafka's aesthetic of desiccation where the touch of the unsayable, as it were, has corroded and dried up language, thus rendering utterance barely possible.

Kafka wants the pure unbroken light—which is the visible, not the objects and forms this light congeals into—to express itself in just this state of its "unbroken-lightness".

He desires to free, as if anticipating Foucault and Deleuze, the visible from the threshold of the sayable and the linguistic. That is the reason why the language of Kafka's prose, despite being made up of elements from the universe of human language, becomes nonsensical the moment one seeks to separate it from the reality of his prose, which this language embodies, to make sense of it as part of the sensible (and representational) human language proper. And yet, it is human language, or at any rate elements taken from it, that Kafka the writer can only resort to. Maurice Blanchot pins down this neurotic impossibility – or dialectic – in Kafka rather accurately: "...all Kafka's texts are condemned to speak about something unique while seeming only to express its general meaning. The narrative is thought turned into a series of unjustifiable and incomprehensible events, and the meaning that haunts the narrative is the same thought chasing after itself across the incomprehensible like the common sense that overturns it. Whoever stays with the story penetrates into something opaque that he does not understand, while whoever holds to the meaning cannot get back to the darkness of which it is the telltale light. The two readers can never meet; we are one, then the other, we understand always more or always less than is necessary. True reading remains impossible."

Thus Kundera's discovery of the comic in Kafka is mistaken. Kafka's novels and parables, to the extent they are linguistic forms and concepts, do certainly produce the comic effect. But that is as incidental as the situations that allude and simultaneously repress their essential constitutive logic. In fact, Kundera contradicts himself, sort of, when he discerns the tragic experience of the characters in Kafka's texts at precisely those points that produce the comic effect for Kafka's readers situated outside the texts. Clearly then, what matter in the Kafkan operation, as far as Kafka himself is concerned, is not the production of the effects of the comic or the tragic but a dialectic that reconciles, obliterates and, thereby transcends, the two. That is the logic Kafka wished to grasp and ventriloquisise, and not the situations or the effects that allude to it only to obscure and repress it.

VI

Kafka's concern, not unlike Marx's, was to grasp and articulate the discursive logic constitutive of human history. We could almost imagine him closing the dialectical circuit—opened by Marx and Engels through the first sentence of The Manifesto of the Communist Party about "the history of all hitherto existing societies" having been "the history of class struggles"—by stating that the history of all hitherto existing human societies has been the inescapable domination of the human being by the equally inescapable law. While Marx's historical optic of the class struggle enabled him to see and envisage the movement of history in terms of a diachronic succession of affirmative, law-unraveling moments that eradicated the law-produced 'beingness' of the human condition and the question of its death to posit the immortality of the trans-human or pure and infinite human-becoming, Kafka's gaze grazed over those struggles to only see the law that is inevitably re-produced in the division of movements into people and the state. For Kafka then, struggle against the law to go beyond it is impossible and meaningless as beyond the law there is more law. Struggle against the law is immanent in Kafka's pessimistic consciousness only as its unhappy unconscious.

Now, to come back to the attraction Kafka held for Benjamin, we would do well to attend to the latter's discovery of the concept of *gestus* in operation in the former's conception of fragments of one's self. That, as far as conceiving the structure of the Marxist-Leninist revolutionary subjectivity goes, is a rather productive opening. *Gestus*, according to Fredric Jameson following French etymology, is both a gesture and an epic. What it means, for Benjamin, and also Brecht, is a particular fragment of a totalised self, embodied in one of its many gestures, and the singular totality of such a fragment whereby the fragment becomes a whole unto itself. We should, however, be attentive to how Kafka positions those fragments vis-à-vis his total self. We should be careful not to conflate what, in my view, is Kafka's consciousness of the gestus—fragments of a self as particularities and/or negative Judaic exceptions to the totality of the manifest self in question that, as a consequence, reinforce that self and its coercive and false totality—and what is immanent in it, which would complete the etymological and also politico-aesthetic dialectic of the concept. To blindly follow Benjamin on Kafka, without recognising the productive tension in the ambiguities of his Judaic-Marxism, could be disastrous. And yet, it's only the encounter with and awareness of such tensions that can enable the illumination of the real trauma in Kafka's soul and aid the production of an authentic revolutionary subjectivity.

7

Media and the Indian State: On the Draft Broadcasting Services Regulation Bill, 2006

The question the Indian Left needs to ask itself most urgently today is whether it would suffice for both its communist and non-communist variants alike to protest against the current government proposal to bring in a broadcasting bill that seeks to limit the operations of a 'free' media? If the intended broadcasting bill is an act of state censorship—which it doubtless is—would it do for the Indian Left to simply see it as such and resist it? In other words, shouldn't the Left, before it takes a definite political position against the proposal, understand the tension within a system of which both the government and the media are integral parts? Only a praxis, which is based on a full comprehension of this systemic tension, can constitute a really interventionist critique of the political economy of the mass media. To put it broadly, the principal concerns of the proposed bill are regulation of market-share of TV companies to purportedly prevent media monopolies from coming up so that homogenisation of opinion can be checked. After all, shouldn't the state in a capitalist democracy like ours be concerned about homogenisation of opinion, and be sensitive to the question of consumer choice? Of course, given the sameness of the content on most of our TV channels, choice is really an illusion. An illusion that is intrinsic to the political economy of the mass media.

Nevertheless, the state's intent in proposing the bill is to putatively articulate the wishes, demands and desires of those social groups, whose concerns find no reflection in, or are undermined and/or contradicted by programming on cable TV channels, which are meant to articulate the ideology of the hegemonic classes. We can sense in this a dialectical tension between two visions of hegemony: one which considers the project of hegemonisation complete. And the other, represented in this case by the government, which thinks that the hegemony of the ruling classes is yet to be conclusively established. So, the current move to bring in the bill is meant to emphasise the fact that the state is as much concerned and bothered about those social groups, which do not 'identify' with the interests of the ruling classes, as the ruling classes themselves as also those who have accepted their ideological hegemony in spite of the fact that their interests do not really converge with those of the ruling classes.

(In fact, when we say that a particular group does or does not identify with the interests of the ruling classes we must qualify that by saying that some groups identify with the interests of the system more than others. After all, capitalism excludes identities, commodities, ideas, cultures to the extent that it orders them in a hierarchy of exchange values. But since things higher up in the hierarchy valorise themselves by transferring value from things, different from them occupying the lower tiers, nothing, from the point of view of the total system, is excluded. We can safely say that capitalism creates hierarchical exclusion of difference even as it includes those differences productively! The bourgeois social formation, which is civil society in common parlance, is constituted by a differential hierarchy of social relations or relations of production.)

So, the government's gesture of proposing the broadcast bill is the gesture of the state, at any rate a sizeable section of it. And constitutive of this gesture is the will of the ruling class—more in a composite ideological sense than in a sociological one because in terms of the latter the ruling class is too internally fragmented and heterogeneous an entity—to hegemonise.

But this tension, or contradiction, between two visions of ideological hegemony of the ruling classes has two possible syntheses, or to borrow from Hegel, "*aufhebung*". The first unity of opposites is obviously the will to hegemonise. It is positive, present and status quoist. The second dialectic, and this should be our main concern, is the will to construct a counter-hegemony, or to be more precise a counter-ideological position. This dialectic—which should be seen as a Marxian overturning of the Hegelian dialectic—is critical, absent and revolutionary.

This will to counter-hegemony is something the genuine working-class forces within the Indian Left will have to extract from the consensus that is being articulated by the government in attempting to bring in legislation to control the free market of the country's free media. The government gesture to bring in the broadcast bill manifests that strand of the will of the ruling class that seeks to hegemonise on the larger political terrain. But it seeks to do so in the name of demand for more choice from among certain social sections lower down in the systemic hierarchy. It is the essence of this demand for more choice from among those social sections, which the Marxists must comprehend. In the scheme of a revolutionary working-class movement, this social demand must be first seen, and then articulated, as being inflected with its negative, counter-ideological and autonomously political desire to reject and unravel the law-constituting gesture of the ruling classes to dominate through ideological hegemony and consensus, or direct coercion, or a combination of both.

Of course, if we were to deal with this within the conceptually segmented domain of the mass media, radical working-class forces should read in this demand for certain kind of TV programmes over others, the sedimented desire to disavow, even challenge, the anti-dialogic orientation intrinsic to the mass media. An orientation that is constitutive of this mass media, thanks to the larger political economy within which it is situated, and which it, at once, facilitates.

Another aspect, which is brought out by this tension between two visions of the ruling classes, is the idea of the autonomisation of the executive. That is, when the state ceases to be a mere executive representative of the ruling class, and becomes an independent entity in itself. Virtually a class for itself, whose decisions are often at variance and in conflict with those of the dominant social class. This happens when polity is faced with, what some Marxists have called the "crisis of representation". This crisis of representation, together with the autonomisation of the executive, has been very evident in India and some other post-colonial Asian nation-states over the past few decades. That is typical of a fascist, and arguably our typically neo-liberal, conjuncture. This crisis of representation happens when the ruling class, and in fact the entire social formation created by and enabling its political economy, is deeply fractured and becomes too internally differentiated to articulate a single cohesive set of interests. In other words, the ideological hegemony of the ruling classes collapses and various contending ideologies, facilitating various sectional interests, come to fore. The executive then steps in to fill the hegemonical vacuum by asserting its independent coercive and administrative role. It does so by playing one class against the other—the bourgeoisie against the proletariat; the petty bourgeoisie against the proletariat; the urban proletariat against its rural counterpart; the petty bourgeoisie against the big bourgeoisie and so on.

This means two things:

a. The government's interests are independent of the interest of all social classes, though it may at times converge with one, at another with the other.

b. Its interests are best served by preserving the current political economy of exchange value and its attendant system of differential inclusion. Consequently, it does everything except unravel the political-economic architectonics of the system.

Let us go back to the broadcast bill in the light of this analysis. To the extent that it seeks to curb the power of an influential section of the dominant classes (the media barons); through executive fiat, it indicates a crisis of representation[1].

At the risk of repeating oneself, it must be stated that the political economy of the modern state, whatever be its form, is constitutive of capitalist valorisation through value transfer. It is this that creates an anti-dialogic, stratified system of productive inclusion. Given this political economy of the state and its various attendant political and social institutions, it would be too much to expect that this tension would, objectively on its own, find a critical resolution. As a matter of fact, the absence of any revolutionary subjective political intervention would most likely resolve it in favour of the status quo: a continuous extension of the hegemonic project of the ruling classes and their ruling ideology.

The revolutionary subjectivity in question will, however, have to be premised on a critical understanding of the political economy and ideological character of the mass media. The Left must understand that this radical subjectivity can come into its own only when it, in being deployed, becomes fully seized of the crisis of representation. Mostly, people resist the state, but without any new paradigm of politics that would seek to understand the state as a function of a certain type of political economy; a certain mode of production; and a certain structure of social relations. Such resistance is, therefore, doomed to be plotted in terms of the status quo of social relations. Thus capturing state power inevitably becomes, for them, an end-in-itself. Every such act of resistance, as a result, ends with some sections of those resisting being absorbed into the state. Those who are not absorbed, again align with those who are preparing to launch a fresh assault against the might of the new state. And thus the vicious cycle continues.

The preponderant tendency of the state is to close itself and exclude others, but it can never do so completely because, objectively, there's a counter-tendency in it to deal with others and include them, if only in a hierarchical fashion and if only to oppress and exploit them in order to transfer value and accumulate capital in all its 'materialised' and 'dematerialised' forms—'cultural capital', 'social capital', political power, money and so forth. The modern state, as a consequence, remains precariously open to challenge. This tension results in it being forced to reflect the demands of those who are lower down in the systemic hierarchy, and who through resistance are trying to move upwards, or towards the centre of it all. But since this demand is articulated by the state; and also because the demand itself is inscribed within the paradigm of modern political power and form of state, even in its resistance it ultimately fails to articulate itself without distorting its counter-ideological, critical essence—the essence, which unconsciously aspires to surpass the distorting mediatory appearance of the prevailing political economy and its ideological, ethico-juridical framework.

So, the UPA government has, through its gesture of proposing the broadcast bill, articulated the so-called *aam aadmi*'s mandate, which demands of it more choice as a consumer. Something that monopolising media houses would obviously be loath to grant them. But this manifest demand and mandate are distorted by the mediation of the politics of state power, its ideologies and institutions, and, most fundamentally, its political economy. It would be the task of revolutionary working-class forces to cut through the clutter and recover what the appearance of this mandate, or this demand has distorted beyond recognition.

Now let us see where this approach of unmasking disguised and alienated political-economic/ideological categories can lead us to in the segmented domain of the mass media. This approach would compel us to analyse the class character of our mass media by figuring out how it deigns to answer the following two questions: is the media meant to aid leisure, and ideological indoctrination and/or skilling of workers by purveying programmes that are passively consumed by them as part and parcel of the reified ritual to socially reproduce themselves? Or, is the mass media a zone where pleasure intersects with critique to produce a radical rupture with the prevailing political economy in both its content and form, which are entwined thoroughly with each other? The one that a revolutionary working-class media would answer in the affirmative is fairly clear.

To understand the fundamental difference between these two visions of the media, we need to simply remember what radical filmmaker Jean-Luc Godard had once said: "TV transmits, while cinema expresses." Here, of course, we must also understand that for Godard TV is the epitome of the bourgeois mass media purveying entertainment, ideologies and skills, while cinema is the supreme expression of what a left-wing cultural-political resistance against such a mass media and its political economy ought to be. For Godard, TV transmits things as they are, and that transmission is meant to be passively recognised, received and consumed as reality by its intended viewers for entertainment and/or 'education'. Cinema, on the other hand, is to express that reality. In other words, it is meant to reflect upon and investigate as to how this reality is constituted. Not just that, it also ends up provoking the audience to participate in that process of reflection and probing. That implies engagement and active participation of the audience. It is this vision of Godard's cinema that has to permeate the Left's cultural-political praxis and its vision of an alternative media.

This kind of cultural politics of resistance has a long and rich legacy.

A. First, of course, is the anti-narrative films of Godard himself. His cinema is known to suddenly rupture the plot and take recourse to various devices and tropes that lead to reflection on the reality that the narrative is seeking to capture or depict.

B. And then, of course, there is Brecht, whose debt Godard has acknowledged time and again, and whose idea and practice of epic theatre did to culture and aesthetics what Marx's did to politics and political economy. In his epic theatre, Brecht sought to alienate the audience from the play, by interrupting its narrative through use of various devices like melodrama, documentary film clips, newspaper cuttings, actual audio recordings of historical events, and so on, in order to unearth and foreground the various processes that constitute and contextualise the reality being depicted in his plays. His intention: to destroy the cathartic consumption of theatre, and the reality it represents, by a passive audience; and provoke that audience into thinking about how reality is historically constituted. His didactic approach was meant to provoke audiences into a dialogue with the producer so that they become active participants in the process of producing the plays, and by extension, the reality outside theatre. Brecht was actually known to have rewritten many of his plays by taking into account the reactions and responses of politically engaged German workers, who were his primary audience.

C. Augusto Boal has taken this Brechtian experiment a step further. His plays of the theatre-of-the-oppressed vintage are produced in a fashion that they provoke the audience to not just reflect on how the narrative is constituted but to actually become part of the play and start participating in it.

D. Filmmaker John Abraham's Odessa film club experiment closer home in Kerala is also another example of how the audiences of cinema can become its producers. Abraham and Odessa made some films successfully with money raised from poor villagers, radical intellectuals and the urban underclass, who often enough also became its cast and supplied their intellectual inputs, too, to the making of those films.

Eventually, however, Odessa has significantly been diminished and it is a pale shadow of its past. This story of Odessa's diminution, however, conceals a moral. A moral that the Left, particularly its cultural political practitioners would do good to absorb and assimilate into their soul. Odessa succeeded only till that time when there was a certain kind of active, left-wing, anti-systemic consensus at work. As soon as that politics went into retreat there were few if any takers for an experiment like the Odessa. This means that cultural-aesthetic practices, like the ones just mentioned, have radical implications in terms of critiquing the prevalent system and its political economy. But those implications have to be actualised through active political praxis.

In the absence of such praxis, these experiments are doomed to be reified into aesthetic-cultural artefacts or forms, by the market's Ricardian logic of value ascription through demand and supply. These experiments become yet another commodity/ideology that the bourgeois mass media includes in its hierarchical jungle of commodities, ideologies and brands.

The Delhi-based Public Service Broadcasting Trust (PSBT) illustrates that point rather well. The PSBT's efforts are geared towards producing short films, both documentaries and features, that the 'public' would 'actually' want to see. It has even gone so far as to produce films by filmmakers drawn from local communities and with participant-actors taken from those communities for those communities as well as others like them. But then, the PSBT is an NGO that looks at people's media and its practices purely in culturalist terms, and is completely divorced from a larger anti-systemic political movement and a political-economic critique of the system. As a result, most of its films and programmes are telecast by the Doordarshan. In other words, the PSBT has to depend on government assistance and subsidy to realise and propagate its purportedly progressive cultural-political vision. In the process, the PSBT programmes, too, have willy-nilly fallen prey to the market's logic of TRP ratings, ad revenue, branding and so forth. Consequently, they are condemned to either survive precariously as government-subsidised artefacts of 'good' culture, which can disappear any moment, just like the National Film Development Corporation (NFDC) of India-sponsored art-house cinema; or they go beyond the pale of leisure-driven mass media to become highly-prized cultural commodities, which are accessed by a privileged few to indulge their supposedly non-utilitarian pleasures. This, according to Theodor Adorno, is precisely how the culture industry creates the reified domains of mass culture and high culture, in which the latter category absorbs everything that is avant-garde and radical, cutting off larger society's access to them, completely defanging them in the process.

That is not to say those 'good cultural' programmes and art-house movies should not be there. (Albeit one must admit that a lot of those NFDC-sponsored films were ponderous, pretentious junk with no real cultural-aesthetic merit and political use.) The point is to ask what is the larger socio-political condition that renders such productions viable, even for the bourgeois mass media.

Such programming can be made viable only by going beyond the market principle of demand and supply; or, more precisely, the split between the active producer and the passive consumer-audience. That would be possible only when media and art are transformed into a de-commodified zone of political resistance and critique of political economy. For, a media that seeks to transform the passive audience into active participant-producer will have to situate itself within, and simultaneously drive, a larger political movement that critiques and seeks to transform the political economy of exchange value and value transfer, which through creation of differential hierarchies privileges oppressive and pedagogic determination of identities over an open dialogue.

Only when such larger politics frames our protest against state censorship or our demand for transparent regulation would they be effective in becoming something more than the effete editorials written by well-meaning leader writers in the mainline press.

Such a political approach also implies the creation of alternative media, and popular cultural-political initiatives, as endeavours that seek to "change the world", not merely "interpret" it. Such initiatives, of which the alternative media would be the instrumentality, would be a movement that intends to heal the producer-consumer breach, and turn passive audiences into active participants in the production of politics, and a horizontal, non-hierarchical society of non-exploitation.

Such cultural-political initiatives must not, however, be confused with reified models of Soviet-style socialist realism and Proletkult. We already have far too much of useless, status quoist *'janwadi'* cultural-political artefacts, like the hoary street theatre, being churned out by various cultural fronts of equally various communist parties. Instead, we would do well to recall what Walter Benjamin says in his 'Author as Producer': "Rather than ask, 'What is the attitude of a work (of art) to the relations of production of its time?' I should like to ask, 'What is its position within them.'" No longer do the cultural-political initiatives of the Indian Left exhibit their original awareness of how their techniques of production, or the forms of representation that resulted from those production processes, are in sync with the socialisation of production that this Left seeks to establish.

The short point, to modify and paraphrase E.P. Thompson, is there can be no culture without struggle. Certainly not for the Marxists.

But this politics of struggle is not just somewhere outside. It is, in fact, situated, on the point where the inside inflects with the outside. The inside, in this case, being people like us: journalists yes, but more importantly media workers.

One is not very experienced in matters organisational and will, therefore, refrain from trying to come up with an organisational plan. But that does not prevent one from emphasising the need for a media workers' organisation, which would contemplate its revolutionary politics in terms of struggles within the place of work of such workers. Such workplace struggles must not focus merely on gaining more wages and/or more time for leisure, but, more importantly in this conjuncture, strive for control over their production process in terms of primarily fighting for an expression of their creativity by seeking to rescue it from the ideologised subjectivity they produce and inhabit while being ground down by the work that subjects them concretely to capital accumulation.

Note: (1) The "crisis of representation" has been explicated well by Karl Marx in his *The Eighteenth Brumaire of Louis Bonaparte*; and later by August Thalheimer and Leon Trotsky while theoretically dealing with the ascendancy of Nazism. The resemblance with India of the past, at least, three decades is uncanny.

8

The Blind Art of the Concrete

> "The real when it has reached the mind, is already not real any more. Our too thoughtful, too intelligent eye."
>
> —Robert Bresson, *Notes on the Cinematographer*

Modern man is cursed with too much of seeing. His every waking moment is suffused and saturated with objects, images, concepts and signs. Such is this profusion of forms that he neither has time nor the inclination to really see what he has to see. And he is oblivious of the virtues of blindness. But can blindness be a virtue? The work of painter Benodebehari Mukherjee—who had a congenitally defective vision, went completely blind in 1957 aged 53, and yet continued to paint for another 23 years—alludes to the visual richness that blindness, and its seeking, can sometimes yield.

There is a lot of variety in Mukherjee's art. But what brings them together is the unity of his aesthetic approach, which sought tirelessly to overcome the world of objects and optical verisimilitude and penetrate their essence. Much of his work, post blindness, is characterised by an almost complete disappearance of opticality, with objects being reduced to their archetypes. Not surprisingly, the human and animal figures of his paper-cuts and collages lack eyes. Two of his post-'57 lithographs—*Curd Seller* and *Kitchen*—are examples of how objects are merely alibis for the artist to explore various interactions among certain essential forms and structures.

But his creations, even before he lost his sight, are marked by a struggle to escape objects and their sheer optical presence. From the very beginning, Mukherjee, as his art indicates, was interested not in things but in relationships among them. Even his self-portraits explore relationships between physiognomy and the character of his inner being.

Mukherjee was also drawn to forces that constitute figures and object rather than the finished 'things' themselves. His *Artist Observing a Frog* is more about capturing the state of two human figures looking at a frog than the visual event per se. This yearning for non-opticality brings Mukherjee close to Anglo-Irish painter Francis Bacon, in spite of their distance in space and tradition. The field of Bacon's paintings, as philosopher Gilles Deleuze has pointed out, lacks depth, and he situates his figures in a way that it appears they are dissolving. Clearly then, Mukherjee, an important member of the Bengal school, was not the only one to have quested after artistic blindness: a metaphor for capturing the unseen in art that is all about seeing. But his loss of vision became a dramatic, physical culmination of this search.

Turkish novelist Orhan Pamuk, who is preoccupied by this aesthetic of 'non-seeing' in his *My Name is Red*, gives a detailed account of the tradition of blindness-seeking among the 12th-13th century masters of Perso-Islamic miniatures. They considered blindness to be the supreme accomplishment of their artistic métier so much so they would often pierce their own eyes with needles specially designed for the purpose. For them, blindness implied the victory of sacred timeless vision over profane human gaze.

The human eye is a compulsive ejaculator of meaning. It is also a repository of pre-conceived notions and ideas. Objects are rendered meaningful only within cages of concepts and forms cast on to them. There is no room for the object to show itself autonomously. Blindness, in such circumstances, is the decimation of the predetermined gaze, if only to set the object free. It is driven by, what French philosopher Gaston Bachelard chose to call, "material imagination" vis-à-vis "formal imagination". The former seeks to shun all formal preconceptions to experience the world directly in its essential and elemental materiality.

Mukherjee's attempt to penetrate the visual realm to get to the essences chimes with Swiss painter Paul Klee's. The deliberate infantilism and primitivity in Klee's paintings allude to the elemental world beyond the realm of our fabricated modern reality. Klee's search for essences was driven by a desire to go back to the roots of the "art image".

Mukherjee's 'blind search' resonates with the ancient mystic traditions of Bengal: of Ramakrishna, the Bauls and Lalanpanthis, Chaitanya and Aatish Dipankara, the 10th-11th century Buddhist monk from erstwhile East Bengal, who journeyed to Tibet to revive Tantric Buddhism. Such mysticism emphasised the dissolution of the individual and his gaze into the world. The idea of non-seeing, which emerged from such mysticism, is not as simple as seeing or saying nothing. It is, in fact, seeing and saying much more than eyes and language can afford. It is faith, not in the sense of submitting to an impenetrable reality, but a state of absolute transparency between the human being and his world so as to preclude any attempt by the former to invade and know the latter.

Mukherjee's decision to paint the 8-foot high, 80-foot long *Life of Medieval Saints* mural on the three walls of Visva Bharati's Hindi Bhavan was not pure chance. The mural, a seamless tapestry of Surdas, Kabir, Ravidas, Tulsidas, Guru Gobind Singh and other medieval Bhakti figures, is an expression of his historical vision that has little to do with the nationalistic grand narratives of his time. In its compositeness, the mural is shot through with the history of Bhakti, not only in the choice of subject but, more importantly, in its vision. History in this mural—which brings together the lives of various medieval saints separated in time and space—is not a mere chronology of events that were seen by human eyes as having unfolded in time. It is an experience, elusive to human eyes, of a timeless emotion. The emotion of "*bhakti*".

In his *Shilpa Jigyasa* (Art's Quest), Mukherjee privileges the world of the primitive anonymous craftsman, ready to dissolve into his tradition, over that of the modern artist with his individual's ego and gaze. However, his return to the 'blind' tradition of the artisan was much too ironical, and thus modern, to replicate the 'repetitiveness' of artisanal craftsmanship in art. It was all about reclaiming the pre-modern ethos of being one with the world.

That helped him free both his memory and imagination from the culturally ingrained habits of seeing and allowed the visual world in his imagination to be mediated by the other four senses. Mukherjee ardently embraced such synaesthesia. He famously distinguished colours by touch after he went blind. His works of that period, even while being visual, have a distinctly tactile quality, too.

'Funes, the Memorious', by Argentine fabulist Jorge Luis Borges (who like Mukherjee continued to work even after he went blind), is an acutely prescient celebration of blindness. The eponymous protagonist of the fable, who is able to remember every small visual detail after a physically crippling accident, is, however, unable to think. That's because thought is generalisation, which entails forgetting much of what we have sensed. Funes, for Borges, is an arch-example of a human being whose imagination and memory are condemned to the prison of the visual. The 'blind' art of Benodebehari Mukherjee, on the other hand, is an intimation of how human beings could one day become more human, and free!

9

In Defence of Hamas

A spectre is haunting Palestine, it is the spectre of Al Qaeda. How else can we explain the near complete abandonment of the Palestinian cause by the international liberal community for which Palestine and its struggle for national self-determination were, till the other day, a never-ending love affair? The erstwhile drivers of the pro-Palestine global liberal consensus blame—allusively if not explicitly—its erosion on the emergence of the radical Islamist Hamas as the principal political agency of their resistance. That, in their reckoning, is completely indefensible at a time when the terroristic depredations of Al Qaeda's pan-Islamism have sought to put the very existence of secular modernity in jeopardy all across the world. Clearly, this liberal perception, permeated as it is by the current international climate of anti-Islamist (even anti-Islamic) opinion, finds nothing wrong in projecting Hamas as a local manifestation of Al Qaeda's reign of internationalist terror and obscurantism.

That has, in the context of the current Israeli attack on the Gaza Strip, meant responses ranging from a spirited advocacy of "Israel's right to defend itself" (the US and the UK governments) and equal condemnation of violence on both sides (various European regimes) to ineffective ritualistic criticism of the Israeli invasion by such die-hard allies of the Palestinian struggle as New Delhi, which has of late found a rather amenable seller of defence hardware in Tel Aviv. And if there can be an abomination greater than the relentlessly brutal assault being unleashed by the Israeli ground, air and naval forces on Gaza Strip, it is constituted by such absurdly heartless, even cynical, reactions. They indicate a wholly unwarranted ideological victory for the Zionist project of occupation and territorial annexation. That the core ideology of Hamas, elected to head the government of Gaza by its inhabitants three years ago, is Islamist has made it easier for the Israeli propaganda machine to render its vile acts of occupation—such as the 30-month-long blockade of Gaza – internationally legitimate. It has helped Tel Aviv suggest to its old and new allies, if such suggestion were necessary, that Hamas's Islamist anti-Israeli position is merely a variant of the virus of pan-Islamist violence that is periodically purveyed by Al Qaeda within their respective geo-political boundaries.

The ideological victory of the Zionist enterprise has, however, more to do with the current global conjuncture than the effectiveness of the Israeli propaganda machine. The eagerness of most 'democratic' nation-states and sizeable sections of their liberal societies to read in the ascendancy of an Islamist Hamas the degeneration of the Palestinian people and their struggle for self-determination stems from this conjuncture, which is characterised by a complete instrumentalisation and institutionalisation of the ideas of liberal-democracy and secularism into an anti-democratic centre of capitalist class power and social domination. What is forgotten, as a consequence, is the true historical origin of the ideology of secularism in the various popular democratic struggles in the western world against institutionalised religion.

It is this subjugation, or shall we say blinding, of secular reason by power that has compelled the liberals of the world to not only equate Hamas's Islamist ideology with that of Al Qaeda's but has also led them to believe that the decision of the majority of Palestinians, particularly those in Gaza, to jettison the secular-nationalist Palestine Liberation Organisation (PLO) for Hamas is a case of wilful fundamentalist aberration. Had the rational capacities of the liberals not been so contaminated by status quoist considerations of power and social privilege, they would have realised that no people—certainly not those who are waging a war of resistance like the Palestinians—choose their political agency, and the ideological idiom and identity that come with it, at their own pleasure and free will. The failure of the global liberal community to ask, let alone figure out, why the Palestinians chose to dump their traditional secular leadership of the PLO, particularly its Al Fatah faction, for an Islamist Hamas, has clearly been due to their ideological inability, if not reluctance, to see the political in terms of the social and vice-versa. In other words, the question of political autonomy, which is what all identitarian struggles for self-determination essentially are, poses the question of cooperative and dialogic social association either directly or implicitly.

What is, however, even more unfortunate is the failure of the global Left forces, in all their national varieties, to insist that their persistent backing for a national self-determination movement like Palestine is precisely because it has served to continuously foreground the aforementioned impulse of social transformation. Instead, their pretext for supporting the Palestinian struggle merely because it is a struggle for national self-determination has, ironically enough, put them on the same page as the liberals who now find Palestine a troubling and embarrassing issue. Such support has, precisely because it has reified the idea of political autonomy and national self-determination, been rendered ineffective. Worse, it has put paid to all hope of engaging the liberal community on its ideologically blinkered, if not politically motivated, perception of Hamas's Islamist politics.

Autonomy, after all, is nothing but a means of seeking true representation of the self by struggling against its false representation by a regime of class domination, which is the logical consequence of a capitalist social order based on the ethic of competition, alienation and difference. Clearly then, autonomy cannot be won unless the order of competitive socialisation is transformed into one of cooperative social association.

In that context, the subjectivities of various movements of political (national, sub-national, caste, race, gender, religious) autonomy, insofar as they pose the question of autonomy and real representation of the concerned socio-political identities without dialectically unfolding the social transformative aspect immanent in them, continue to be articulated by the bourgeois logic of competitive socialisation. It is, therefore, hardly surprising that political autonomy and self-determination are, as far as such subjectivities are concerned, mostly articulated in terms of sovereignty—a bourgeois notion of competitive socio-politics, which philosopher Georges Bataille explained as the complete invasion of the other by the self. Yet, it would be difficult to deny that such subjectivities at their moment of resistance—against their experience of social domination and false representation—unconsciously posit the objective struggle for decimation of the bourgeois order of competitive socialisation, and its transformation into a domain of free association.

The reason why the PLO's leadership no longer finds too many takers among Palestinians, especially the preponderantly poor population of Gaza, is not only because it has ceased to posit such free associative and dialogic mode of socialisation but also because it has been actively blocking and undermining it. To see the rise of Hamas as an outcome of the corruption and venality of the PLO—manifest most acutely in the latter's post-Oslo Palestinian Authority (PA)—is to merely put the problem in a moral frame. In real political terms, this venality of the PLO is no more than a manifestation of the emergence of a privileged class within the larger Palestinian society. Members of traditional propertied classes among Palestinians together with the new intellectual-political elite, chiefly of PLO and Al Fatah vintage, comprise this new class. This social phenomenon has, at the political level, found expression in the institutionalisation of the PLO and its version of the Palestinian movement. It is no coincidence that West Bank, which is home to Palestinians who have much better access to socio-economic entitlements such as education, employment, health, and various civic amenities both in quantitative and qualitative terms, is the base of PLO, PA and their secular Palestinian identity. On the other hand, Gaza, inhabited principally by pauperised and proletarianised Palestinians, has come to be the centre of Hamas's politics of uncompromising anti-Israeli resistance.

It is in this context that Hamas's refusal to expressly eschew its stated position of not recognising Israel's right to exist must be examined. The Oslo Accords between Tel Aviv and Yasser Arafat's PLO in 1993 led to the Palestinians, under PLO's leadership, recognising Israel's right to exist as an independent nation in exchange for Tel Aviv's acceptance of Palestinian national self-determination through interim self-government arrangements within the pre-1967 boundaries. The acceptance of those boundaries meant, in practical terms, accepting only the two territories of West Bank and Gaza Strip as Palestinian. It is these accords that culminated in the setting up of the PA. But in real terms, Oslo has meant Palestinian self-determination only on paper as Israel has been engaged in gerrymandering "facts on the ground" by constantly pushing more and more Jewish settlers way beyond the real pre-1967 borders and deep into territories recognised as Palestinian by the Oslo Accords. That Israel would need to continuously violate the spirit of Oslo in this fashion is fairly clear. Its Zionist raison d'etre of Eretz Yisrael, the "land of Israel" for all Jews of the world, will keep inducing it to acquire more and more land for building new settlements for Jews, who continue to pour in from every corner of the world to seek the fulfilment of this founding promise of Israel.

The PA, especially under Arafat's successors Ahmed Querie and Mahmoud Abbas, not only acquiesced in this brazen molestation of Oslo by Israel but even facilitated the violation by using both its security forces and armed Al Fatah fighters to keep Palestinian protesters, in Gaza (till the election of Hamas) and West Bank, at bay. That Abbas and his PLO crowd have watched, more or less silently, even as Tel Aviv has mounted its atrocities in Gaza ever since a Hamas government pushed PA out of there, is entirely of a piece with the PLO's post-Oslo stance.

The PLO's collaboration in this Israeli project of subverting the spirit of Oslo is both a cause and consequence of preserving the social interests of the privileged Palestinian classes in West Bank. The compliant collaboration of the PA with Israel has not only meant that the much better access of its privileged Palestinians to socio-economic entitlements and concomitant socio-political power, vis-à-vis the Palestinian poor of Gaza, is ensured. It has also helped this elite to fend off the political challenge of the toiling classes, rallied behind Hamas, through the instruments of Israeli occupation.

That, however, does not mean the PLO and the PA have stopped posing their versions of a self-determined Palestinian identity vis-à-vis the Israeli occupation. But their recent 'struggle', which has inevitably turned out to be an apology of the concerted resistance movements it had earlier conducted, poses the identity of the privileged Palestinian class in a spirit of competition with regard to the privileged sections among the Jews, whose interests are embodied in the ideological-political project called Israel. As a result, the PLO-PA 'struggle' against Israel is merely geared towards enhancing the social position of the Palestinian elite within the stratified global political-economic order as it obtains to in the region. Clearly, the existential impulse of the Palestinian identity currently posed by the PLO-PA is that of reinforcing the capitalist logic of competitive socialisation. That collaboration with Israel takes precedence, for the PLO-PA, over its assertion of Palestinian autonomy indicates the quest of the privileged Palestinian classes for self-determination is essentially a bourgeois competitive enterprise to further their social domination. That, needless to say, has only reinforced the hegemony of global capitalism, and its Yankee-Zionist moment in the region.

Hamas's refusal to abandon its stated position questioning Israel's right to exist is, in that context, a repudiation of Oslo, which in reality has paved the way for collaboration between Tel Aviv and the PLO-PA. That has conferred a fig leaf of legitimacy on continued Israeli occupation, directed at denying the Palestinian underclass its real autonomy, but also enabled the social domination of the underprivileged Palestinians by their own social elite under the PLO-PA's wing. To that extent, the Hamas-led resistance in Gaza for Palestinian national self-determination has, at this juncture, been both a struggle against socio-political domination and the bourgeois logic of competitive socialisation that has engendered it.

All that does not, however, still explain why an agency of the Palestinian underclass, which is ranged against the collaborationist apparatus of Israeli occupiers and a Palestinian elite, would need to abandon its original secular-nationalist ideological idiom for a more puritan variety of Islam. And this question cannot be answered unless the secular-nationalism of the PLO, which was rejected after it became the ideology of a political institution of a privileged Palestinian elite, is located within the ideological-social space of Islam in the West Asian, especially the Palestinian, region. Islam has been the dominant indigenous cultural form in that region and all stirrings of enlightenment among its predominantly Arab peoples have been in its language. Arab-Christians have adopted the modern nationalist discourse, which has been articulated in this specific form of Islamic language, as much as the Arab-Muslims. The secular-nationalist ideology of the Palestinian national struggle under the PLO can be traced to the late 19th century *Nahada* (Arab Renaissance), when Islam was read against its traditional grain to articulate an absolutely modern idea of Arab nationalism against the Turkish Ottomans, whose imperial caliphate had then embodied the traditional idea of institutionalised pan-Islamism. It should, therefore, be clear that the secular nationalism of the Palestinian resistance under the PLO was not secular in the conventionally understood western sense of the term. It was imbued with Islam, albeit a liberal and inclusive variety of it. The ideological shift of the poor Palestinians—who now constitute the vanguard of the Palestinian struggle for self-determination—towards a relatively more traditionalist and pietistic conception of the religion must, therefore, be seen as a movement within the Islamic ideological space, away from its more liberal end, precisely because this liberalism has lost its earlier inclusiveness. To claim this was the only alternative the proletarianised Palestinians of Gaza had, considering that an effective working class force was absent in Palestine would be like stating the obvious.

And yet, it would be grossly inaccurate to equate the Hamas-led Palestinian struggle with Al Qaeda's international jehad merely because both articulate their politics in the idiom of religious Islam. Hamas's so-called radical Islam is, clearly, an organic language of protest, resistance and autonomy against socio-political domination by a foreign state and an institutionalised, secular local elite. Al Qaeda, on the other hand, posits its Islam as an anti-dialogic institution that needs to be imposed on the entire world in the form of an international caliphate. In fact, Al Qaeda's institutionalised religion is no different from the institutionalised anti-democratic secularisms of modern capitalist powers it seeks to displace. Clearly, Al Qaeda's struggle against capitalist liberal modernity is a competitive struggle of a section of disgruntled Gulf Arab elite funded by petro-dollars against other sections of that same elite and their socio-political allies within the stratified hegemony of global capitalism. Al Qaeda is a force of fascist reaction, Hamas the harbinger of dogged resistance and hope.

10

Sri Lanka: Genocide and Other Majoritarian Falsehoods

Majoritarian chauvinism is almost always seen as a natural, if not a fitting, response to fascistic tendencies within a minority community. Sri Lanka has been no exception. The manner in which the triumphal advance of the island-nation's armed forces into the northern bastion of the Liberation Tigers of Tamil Eelam (LTTE) have been welcomed the world over, and particularly in India, indicates this has indeed become established wisdom. Buoyed by the current discourse on terrorism, the global opinion seems to have internalised the idea that violence cannot be immoral or unjust as long as it emanates from the state. And yet there could not be a crueler joke at this moment than to offer the imminent victory of the Sri Lanka Army (SLA) over the LTTE as hope of redemption to Tamils of the island-nation. Not only would such a victory weigh heavily against them by reinforcing the oppressive status quo and its configurations of majoritarianised socio-political power; it would completely obscure the origins of authoritarian and bonapartist tendencies among Tamils in the institutionalised Sinhala majoritarianism and the larger fascist conjuncture of Sri Lankan society.

Is New Delhi being naïve when it continually expresses its concern for the civilian Tamil population of northern Sri Lanka even as it extends complete 'moral' support to the SLA's operations against the Tigers' apparatus of "terror"? The two simply do not sit together. Sri Lanka President

Mahinda Rajapaksa's assertion that the SLA has been extremely careful in preventing collateral damage while mounting and carrying out successful military assaults on the political-military bases of the LTTE is, in that context, entirely disingenuous. And the only claim that exceeds such cant is Colombo's declaration that it would implement the country's 13th constitutional amendment for devolution of more powers to the northern province, once the LTTE has been wiped out, to enable the majority Tamil population of that province to realise its aspiration for greater autonomy. For, it is precisely the repeated denial of such autonomy to the Tamils by the majoritarian Sinhala polity and state that jump-started the Tamil separatist insurgency and civil war in Sri Lanka. It is kind of hard to believe that the island Tamils, who failed to wrest such autonomy from the Sinhala state during the heyday of their politics, would be bestowed with such autonomy at a time when they have no real and effective political agency left.

If Colombo does, indeed, effect such devolution, it would be no more than a top-down political manoeuvre, which instrumentalises Tamil autonomy and renders it purely formal. In other words, such institutionalised autonomy would barely be a chimera of the political autonomy the Sri Lankan Tamil struggle, both in its federalist-constitutionalist phase and its more radical separatist-nationalist moment, had sought to accomplish. This struggle for autonomy, albeit articulated by the bourgeois logic of competitive national sovereignty, had potentially posed the question of transforming the unequal configurations of social power and entitlements and their institutionalisation in a Sinhala majoritarian state into a more cooperative, dialogic and egalitarian socio-economic formation and, therefore, a more democratic and participatory state formation. The autonomy the Rajapaksa regime would deliver to the northern Tamils—whose vigorous political struggle for self-determination has almost entirely been exterminated—after it militarily vanquishes the LTTE, would leave the institutionalised structures of majoritarian power, and the unequal social order it is constitutive of, intact. Such autonomy would, therefore, at best create a new strata of Tamil political elite, which would be accommodated by its Sinhala counterparts in a spirit of class collaboration within the existing structures of socio-economic privilege and socio-political power. Meanwhile, the condition of the pauperised Tamil working class—which is already quite handicapped by the disappearance of the vigorous Tamil nationalist struggle and the non-emergence of a real proletarian movement—would only get worse.

That, after all, is exactly what Colombo has achieved in the name of devolution in the other Tamil majority province in the east, which was once also a hotbed of LTTE activity. The Tamils who comprise the supposedly more autonomous provincial government are essentially renegade LTTE elite, including Colonel Karuna, who was Vellupillai Prabhakaran's eastern satrap till he fell out with the Tiger supremo in what was no more than a power struggle between two sections of the LTTE elite. That this government has delivered neither democracy nor equity to the eastern province is amply indicated by reports of a new power struggle having taken root within the breakaway LTTE faction and its government with the resulting violence spilling over into its wider Tamil-dominated society.

It is nobody's case, though, that the LTTE is a paragon of national-liberationist and revolutionary virtues. The organisation has become, for its Tamil constituency, a fount of institutionalised military oppression. It has, as a consequence, undermined the very concept of Tamil political autonomy it claims to be fighting for. The question, in such circumstances, is who will decimate and displace the LTTE and how will it be done? To assume, as many including even some liberal sympathisers of Sri Lankan Tamils have, that it does not matter at this juncture if this task of eliminating the authoritarian organisation is accomplished by the security forces of the majoritarian Sinhala state is not only politically misplaced, but ethically troublesome too. The modality of politics constitutive of the ongoing anti-LTTE operation of the SLA sees not only the competitive struggle posed by the LTTE-led Tamil political elite against the Sinhala elite as a threat to the latter's superior position within the socio-political hierarchy in the region, it even sees whatever is left of the non-LTTE Tamil nationalist impulse rooted in the Tamil working class as a challenge to its position and the hegemony of competitive and stratified capitalist socialisation it embodies. The overrunning of Killinochi, the LTTE's administrative capital, by the SLA and the current fight to the finish it is waging against Tiger guerrillas in the jungles of Mullaithivu are, therefore, part of a deliberate military-political strategy to destroy not only the LTTE but also, in the bargain, crush all genuine aspirations for Tamil autonomy and empowerment and the concomitant potential desire to shift the paradigm of socialisation from competition and domination to cooperative socio-economic association and socio-political dialogue.

To not recognise this modality of anti-LTTE Sinhala politics, even as the LTTE is castigated for its reactionary and authoritarian strain of Tamil nationalism renders 'fascism' into an abstract, one-dimensional moral category and fails to locate it within the larger conjunctural dynamic of capitalism and its institutionalised structures of power. The LTTE's ossification into a parallel state indicates the transformation of a section of the leadership of the Tamil nationalist resistance into a bureaucratised political elite. This transition, which occurs in all movements for political autonomy, has in this case underscored the failure of a section of the Tamil resistance movement to articulate, not merely subjectively but also objectively, the dialectical interplay between the social and the political. All struggles for political autonomy, whether proletarian or national-liberationist, aim to capture state power. Such seizure of state power is, however, not an end in itself. It is the first step towards reconfiguring institutionalised political power in a fashion that renders the state formation more participatory so that the qualitative and quantitative distribution and circulation of resources, which are constitutive of the differential of socio-political power, are also radically altered to yield a more egalitarian and less exploitative socio-economic order. An anti-LTTE critique and political struggle, which ought to have emerged from within the wider Sri Lankan Tamil society, would have sought to redress the failure of the Tamil nationalist movement on that count. The struggle, which would have sought to displace the LTTE, would not have implied a criticism of the Tigers' will to capture state power as it would have attempted to do pretty much the same. Rather, it ought to have spelt rejection of the LTTE on behalf of the dispossessed and disenfranchised majority of the Sri Lankan Tamils for its unwillingness to reconfigure hierarchised structures of social power into a maximally democratic, cooperative and dialogic socio-political domain. This struggle, needless to say, would have had to be against the LTTE and the new Tamil political elite it embodies without giving up the larger Tamil resistance against Sinhala chauvinism.

In fact, the continuous forging of alliances among various Tamil nationalist outfits, their frequent disintegration into mutually warring factions, and splits within organisations—ever since the days of the formation of the Tamil United Front in 1972, the Tamil United Liberation Front in 1976 and right up until the mid-'80s - was precisely the churn that resulted from such struggles within the movement among the champions of a Tamil elite constantly in the making and the proponents of Tamil underclasses. That this churn eventually came to an end with the LTTE managing to successfully eradicate all opposition to its Thermidorian ascendancy within the Tamil national movement in Sri Lanka is largely responsible for the current predicament of the Sri Lankan Tamils where they are condemned to choose between two forms of ethno-nationalist authoritarianism.

That the Tamil movement for political autonomy has been a nationalist movement makes this predicament doubly difficult to beat, especially for the Tamil working class. Isaac Deutscher had, in an interview on the Palestinian-Israeli conflict to the New Left Review in 1967, said: "...even in the revolutionary phase each nationalism has its streak of irrationality, an inclination to exclusiveness, national egoism and racism." He could well have been speaking about Tamil nationalism.

There is absolutely no doubt that both the initial federalist movement for Tamil autonomy, under the leadership of S J V Chelvanayagam's Tamil Federal Party, and the violent Tamil nationalist separatism into which it was subsequently transformed, through two decades of the recalcitrant rise and spread of Sinhala-Buddhist chauvinism, were largely centred on a revanchist conception of the indigenous Tamil community's royalist and feudal past in the northern and eastern parts of the island. And yet it would be equally difficult to deny that the emergence of such politics was entirely on account of the Tamils' political disenfranchisement, socio-economic dispossession and cultural marginalisation—various moments of a singular political-economic manoeuvre—effected by an extremely repressive and supremacist Sinhala polity. Merely because native Tamil elites of Sri Lanka's north and east experienced the institutionalised socio-economic marginalisation and political disempowerment of their community as an erosion of their traditional privileges, and have articulated it thus, does not mean that the Sinhala ruling classes have not systematically repressed and pauperised them. Legislation such as the Official Language Act, 1956, which proclaimed Sinhalese as the sole official language, the enactment of a Sinhala-supremacist Constitution in 1972 that made Buddhism into a de-facto state religion, not to speak of various legal and extra-legal measures (riots and pogroms) to socio-economically hold down the Tamils, are examples of how Sinhala majoritarianism has been the local ideological manifestation of the capitalist political economy of economic exploitation, social oppression and political domination. In such circumstances, Sri Lankan Tamil nationalism, which is objectively located in a social group that aspires to liberate itself from socio-political domination and economic marginalisation, cannot be rejected just because its ideological provenance and political tenor have been revanchist and elitist respectively. To quote Deutscher again: "The nationalism of the people in semi-colonial or colonial countries, fighting for their independence must not be put on the same moral-political level as the nationalism of conquerors and oppressors. The former has its historic justification and progressive aspect which the latter has not."

True, the failure of Sri Lanka's native Tamils to take up the cause of the Indian origin Tamil plantation workers of the central highlands, when they were repatriated to India in 1964 after the major anti-Tamil pogrom of 1958 in the Sinhala-dominated areas, was precisely on account of this elitist and revivalist orientation of the Tamil autonomy movement. And yet that would only be a partial telling of the story. Most of the blame for the brutal marginalisation, and repatriation (read expulsion) of this indentured community of Tamil workers should be laid on the doors of the Communist Party of Ceylon and the Ceylon Workers' Party: working class organisations that had been the principal political agency of those central highland Tamils till they gradually began allowing their politics, together with that of other Sinhala liberals, to be by and large subsumed by the right-wing nationalism of the Sinhala elite. That, needless to say, virtually extinguished the fundamentally secular and social transformative politics of the Tamil indentured labourer community. A politics that could have emerged as a more progressive and ecumenical alternative to both the LTTE's brand of authoritarian nationalism and the majoritarian chauvinism of the Sinhala ruling classes.

Besides, it would be grossly inaccurate to trace the genealogy of LTTE's autocratic vision of Tamil nationalism to the elitist ideological moorings of the original movement for Tamil autonomy. The emergence of revolutionary guerrilla groups through the mid-'70s to the early '80s, which either avowed a left-wing nationalist or a Maoist position, shows that nationalism of Sri Lankan Tamils had progressed beyond its elitist beginnings in the quest for federal autonomy towards a politics that sought to envisage national self-determination in terms of a larger project of militant social transformation. That groups such as the Tamil Eelam Liberation Organisation, Eelam Revolutionary Organisation of Students, People's Liberation Organisation of Tamil Eelam and Eelam People's Revolutionary Liberation Front were eventually wiped out by the LTTE, which had in the meantime degenerated into a bureaucratised and institutionalised cabal of a new Tamil political elite, was as much on account of the tactical, political-military failure of those revolutionary nationalist groups vis-à-vis the LTTE, as the effective support the LTTE elite received from the Indian ruling classes (state) in their collaborative competition against the Sinhala ruling elite on one hand, and the revolutionary nationalist Tamil impulse on the other. All that, however, changed with the arrival of the Indian Peacekeeping Force (IPKF) in Sri Lanka in 1987. The war the IPKF waged against the LTTE signaled a shift in the axis of competitive struggle among various configurations of the regional elite within the larger stratified capitalist hegemony in the region. Clearly, the Indian state was now collaborating with the Sinhala elite in a bid to not only prevent the LTTE's new political elite from emerging as a force to reckon with within the stratified capitalist order of the region, but to also exterminate all revolutionary Tamil nationalist impulses that could pose a challenge to the hegemony that underpinned this order. The support the current Indian government has been extending to the Sri Lankan Army's relentless advance into Tiger country, even as it joins Colombo to pay lip-service to the well-being of Tamil civilians "trapped by the LTTE fighters" in the jungles of Mullaithivu, is of a piece with this decades-old Indian imperialistic enterprise of preserving the existing structure of socio-political stratification in the region and the capitalist hegemony that engenders it. It is probably not naïveté after all.

11

Fascism in its Liberal Womb

There can be nothing more precarious in the life of a liberal-democracy than the evacuation of politics from law. India currently faces precisely such a crisis, evident in the emergence of Hindutva terror, its insidious denial by mainstream 'social' and political outfits of the Hindu Right and, ironically, even the terms in which the secularist camp has sought to counter their propaganda. It is, in fact, the liberal-secular aspect of the problem that is, at once, most interesting and disturbing.

A sizeable section of Indian liberals has, in ascribing double standard to the sangh parivar that has been maligning the Maharashtra anti-terrorism squad's investigation into the September 29 Malegaon blasts, unwittingly come to share the political-ideological assumptions of Hindutva. Sangh parivar outfits, after having viciously opposed all attempts to call into question the fairness and neutrality of police-investigative procedures into acts of what they call "jehadi terror", have suddenly done a U-turn to accuse the Maharashtra ATS of being politically pliable and its line of probe into the Malegaon explosions ideologically compromised. Even the BJP has, as is its equivocal wont, carefully allowed only some of its senior leaders to lend their voices to this pernicious cultural-nationalist chorus.

Yet, accusing Hindutva groups of hypocrisy and double standard would close more democratic doors than open them. Such accusation may or may not help the anti-BJP forces score electoral brownie points now. But they would certainly discredit, in advance, all criticism and questioning of state institutions for all times to come. To get caught in debates about the desirability of interrogating and criticising state institutions is to miss the point.

What matters is whether critical interrogation of state instrumentalities, or the criticism of such criticism, has been prompted by the political desire to render the state and its institutions accountable to a people who embody the values of our Constitution. That would be democracy. The politics of Hindutva, which seeks to make state institutions amenable to the will of an a priori mass at odds with the radical democratic principles of self-determination through a process of continuous critical unravelling of closed institutions, is majoritarianism. And yet in the absence of a politics that would enable people to make that distinction, democracy and majoritarianism are easily conflated. Sangh parivar organisations have accomplished precisely that with great success.

In such circumstances, direct organisational links between the Malegaon accused and the sangh parivar, even if they do exist, are of little consequence. What is both important and indisputable is their ideological kinship. That, more than any organisational tie, is a characteristic feature of fascism.

Fascism cannot, however, be effectively battled as long as its opponents remain unaware of the gaps in the legalistic discourse and practice of liberal democracy. It is in those fissures that the pestilence of fascism, irrespective of whether it takes the form of Islamism or Hindutva, silently breeds. That said, it would be ideologically troublesome and politically perilous for us here in India to tar the two forms of fascism—Hindutva and Islamism—with the same brush. If anything, such an equation would only reinforce the problematic legal, anti-political praxis of liberal democracy.

We need to distinguish one from the other, even at the risk of appearing undesirably divisive. For, in the long run, more harm than good would be done if this difference is obscured now for some tenuous gains on the Hindu-Muslim brotherhood front. The point of this comparison is not to legitimise the idea of 'lesser evil'. The point is to recognise the difference in political structures and processes constitutive of each of those strains of terror, if only to come up with a composite political alternative to the larger problem of civic violence of which both Islamism and Hindutva have become indivisible halves. There is absolutely no doubt that both the Islamists and the footsoldiers of Hindutva seek to close the democratic space through their terroristic campaigns, both covert and overt. But what is more germane is that while the former seeks to subvert liberal democracy by challenging it from the vantage point of opposition and resistance, the latter strives towards the same goal by using the language of liberal democracy and manipulating its institutions.

The recognition of this difference in methods is crucial because it serves to illuminate a rather intractable problem posed by demographics that liberal democracy cannot discern, leave alone resolve, as long as it posits itself in legal-ethical terms. The right to life of a citizen—the foundational liberty on which the edifice of liberal democracy stands—has implicit in its conception the idea of protecting a particular form of material and cultural life from elements that endanger it. The legal-ethical paradigm of liberal democracy entirely precludes the political-agnostic approach, which historicises the normative liberal-democratic idea of citizen and his eligibility of rights as an abstraction of a certain (insurgent) moment of transformative politics seeking real human autonomy. Such historicised engagement with liberal democracy would leave us with no choice but to seek to break with its ethical-legal framework if only to remain true to its impulse (read logic) of continuously seeking concrete human autonomy. The absence of such a reading—which is the default position to which the ethical-legal paradigm of liberal democracy inevitably obtains to—ends up upholding and defending the sovereignty of a certain form of life that is created solely by the majority community and accessed either only by its members or those among others who accept the ideological hegemony of such a qualified form of life, which constitutes the biopolitical horizon of the liberal-democratic polity. All others become, on this terrain of biopolitics, bearers of a form of bare life—as opposed and inferior to the qualified life form—whose sovereignty a liberal democratic state is not only not obliged to defend but is actually also tasked to hold at bay through repression because it threatens the sovereignty of the life of the citizen.

In such circumstances, a citizen eligible for his rights is one who enjoys the entitlements that enables him to the qualified form of cultural and material life, which comes to characterise the national mainstream. Those who cannot, or do not, access such entitlements are obviously not eligible to be rightful citizens. The paradox is that such biopolitical entitlements can be accessed by those who do not have it by invoking rights, even as those rights are denied to them precisely because they do not have the entitlements that would qualify them as citizens. This problem cannot, clearly, be resolved within the ethical-legal and status quoist paradigm that liberal democracy posits but only through a politics that seeks to break/reconfigure/redistribute the status quo of entitlements by replacing legislation with a political movement for socio-economic transformation.

The absence of such a political imaginary—of which the hegemonic establishment of the ethical-legal discourse of liberal democracy is the other dialectical half—virtually legitimises majoritarianism, even as it frames the opposition of social groups either excluded or repressed in that status quo in some kind of minoritarian idiom, which is simultaneously rendered illegitimate. That is the reason why fascism, when it is manifest as Hindutva in our country, is seen by a whole clutch of committed liberal democrats through a prism tinged with partial, if not total, acceptability. The same bunch, not surprisingly, displays no such ambivalence while characterising Islamist fascism as the greatest evil of our times. There is a desperate need for a more agnostic (read political) approach to liberal democracy. Nothing short of that would help us transcend our fascist status quo and the liberal democratic discourse that makes this enormity possible.

12

Lalgarh beyond Maoism, Maoism beyond Lalgarh

In politics, the truth is almost always counter-intuitive. In this realm—where the art of the possible intersects in strangely unexpected ways with the science of the impossible—ominous portents of anarchy often conceal messianic promises of deliverance. Lalgarh, today, is perhaps the starkest symbol of this confounding cocktail, which has come to characterise the polity of Left Front-ruled West Bengal. But the violent upheavals, which have been rocking this tribal-dominated village of West Midnapore over the past several months, are unlikely to yield any meaning as long as socio-political violence continues to be envisaged as a moral question. If anything, such a moral approach would only produce counter-productive programmes and practices that would inexorably push politics further down the hopeless pit of a degenerate status quo.

Whether the Lalgarh movement constitutes an unconscionable disruption of social peace, or is a legitimate popular upsurge cannot be conclusively determined unless the objective political condition and logic of that movement and its subjective ideological orientation, especially with regard to the adoption of violence as an instrumentality of politics, is accurately accounted for. What clearly distinguishes the Lalgarh uprising from other apparently similar violent incidents and agitations that have scarred West Bengal over the past few years, and which have registered a sudden spurt in the aftermath of the resounding victory of the Trinamool Congress-Congress alliance over the CPI(M)-led Left Front (LF) in the 15th Lok Sabha elections, is that the calculus of competitive electoral politics has had absolutely no bearing on the movement. The reason why electoral considerations have figured rather significantly in most other zones of unrest in the state is because the strife in those zones has been ignited mainly by the collapse of the CPI(M)-led LF's well-oiled and calibrated network to differentially distribute political patronage by way of governance. This has particularly been the case in areas such as Nandigram and Singur where the main battle has been against acquisition of farmland for industrial development.

The struggle for patronage is essentially a competitive struggle that has no concern loftier than that of conserving and progressively concentrating positions constitutive of a structurally inequitable and undemocratic status quo. That does not, however, mean the distress and disaffection caused by the collapse of such patronage, which is all that is there by way of governance in LF-ruled West Bengal, is not real. The trouble is the political idiom in which such genuine anxieties are being articulated is, in being shaped by the all-pervasive regime of patronage politics, thoroughly competitive. That has inevitably rendered such mass movements susceptible to all sorts of cynical manoeuvres and manipulations.

The popular eruption in Lalgarh, on the other hand, has been driven by no such competitive consideration precisely because the remote tribal belt of which it is a part has had little or no patronage network to begin with.

The insurgency of the Lalgarh population has been shaped by its experience of a state that has registered its presence in the area through the brutal effectiveness of its repressive security apparatuses but has been absent as an organic expression of the will of the people and an efficient purveyor of emancipatory social development and vital public goods. Clearly, the problem there is not, as many seem to believe, the absence of the state but its existence as a completely alienated and foreign entity. Those being the objective conditions for the emergence and expansion of the Lalgarh movement, it is highly unlikely that it is capable of positing, or even articulating, anything other than a transformative critique of the alienated and repressive state, and the intrinsically competitive and hierarchical socio-economic order that engenders it.

And that is precisely why the temptation to classify the Lalgarh uprising as a tribal identity movement, driven by the ideology of some organic notion of autonomous communitarianism, should be resisted. The majority population of Lalgarh is doubtless tribal but the anti-competitive orientation of their struggle, thanks to the objective politico-economic conditions that have shaped them, serves to completely invert the competitive logic of identitarian movements, which always articulate their politics in supremacist terms of ethno-cultural pride and domination. Put simply, the Lalgarh movement clearly manifests characteristic features of a working-class struggle.

The People's Committee against Police Atrocities-led revolt, which was sparked seven months ago by a repressive combing operation launched by the West Bengal police in Lalgarh and surrounding areas in response to a Maoist mine attack on the chief minister's cavalcade, has steadily morphed into a more proactive and comprehensive struggle for a fundamental transformation of the socio-political structure. That has yielded a two-pronged movement of resistance and reconstruction. It is, therefore, no accident that the PCPA, which has been leading the militant mass movement against the West Bengal government in Lalgarh, is now also at the forefront of an incipient social reconstruction programme for the enforcement of a cooperative and democratic management of resources and rudimentary public services such as healthcare developed by the local community itself.

That the CPI(M)-led West Bengal government, infamous for its autocratic ways, was extremely cagey until a few weeks ago to crack down on the movement was largely due to its mass insurrectionary character. In Lalgarh, violence against state apparatuses has not been launched by a clearly identified group acting on behalf of an oppressed but largely passive population. Instead, it has been an expression of disaffection and opposition by a population entirely insurgent against a repressive state and the oppressive socio-economic order it protects and perpetuates. Even the guerrilla operations carried out by Maoists in the area and its neighbourhood have become a seamless extension of this insurrection, which inevitably enjoys wide-ranging local legitimacy and has some serious moral standing, vis-à-vis the rest of the state. It is this legitimacy, which derives from an assertion of popular sovereignty, that had kept West Bengal's Stalinist dispensation away from open repressive manoeuvres for so long. That it had burnt its fingers in Nandigram, where its cadre together with the state police had attempted a scorched-earth operation a couple of years ago, has only compounded its diffidence on that score.

After all, a modern state formation, no matter how repressive, has to always act in the name of protecting popular sovereignty. But in an insurrectionary situation, like the one in Lalgarh, the sovereignty vested normatively in the state is clearly in conflict with actual sovereignty on the ground. In such circumstances, the state, if it cracks down on the movement, runs the grave risk of losing all formal legitimacy it enjoys as the keeper of people's sovereignty. In fact, it is the state or the government that, in such a situation, comes to be seen as an external threat to the sovereignty of the people, and the violent insurrection of the latter against the state pushes it and its laws into a situation of crisis. That renders the legal-illegal dichotomy problematic and consequently makes it difficult for the state to legitimately monopolise violence to crush popular movements in the name of combating anti-sovereign lawlessness and insurgency. That is a risk the CPI(M)-led LF could ill-afford at a moment when the electoral drubbing it has received in

West Bengal signals significant erosion of its moral-political standing.

The Lalgarh movement could, nevertheless, hardly have gone on for ever without inviting the wrath of the ruling classes of West Bengal and India. The only way a movement like that could possibly evade state repression and keep itself alive and kicking is through continuous political growth accomplished through a relentless process of engagement and integration with concerns, anxieties and disaffections in other areas and sectors of the state. Yet, an unpardonable tactical blunder on the part of the Maoists, who indisputably have a sizeable numerical presence in the PCPA, has cleared the way for the West Bengal government to unleash repression on the Lalgarh movement sooner rather than later. The recent claims by various senior Maoist leaders and activists that the PCPA was a front of the underground outfit, which was controlling and running the show in Lalgarh, has given the repressive arms of both the LF government of West Bengal and the Centre the alibi they had been waiting for. The West Bengal government has, over the past few days, turned proactive and has been dispatching contingents of heavily armed police and central paramilitary forces to Lalgarh to crush the popular uprising. That the LF dispensation has suddenly regained its usual repressive element is because it knows the police operation in Lalgarh would now be widely perceived as a legitimate measure taken by the state to protect popular sovereignty from Maoists and some sections of the local community they have 'bamboozled'.

The Maoists, thanks to their doctrinaire programmatic commitment to agrarian revolution and the concomitant tactical emphasis on guerrilla struggles exclusively in tribal and rural areas of the country, have failed to focus on developing large-scale popular movements in the semi-urban and urban areas. Their time-worn approach of encirclement of cities by people's army raised from the countryside has, willy-nilly, militarised their politics, what with their roving guerrilla squads carrying out dramatic raids on behalf of a rural population they have barely organised. That, among other things, has ensured their politics enjoys little concrete ideological-political support among working people in Indian cities. As a result, it has been rather easy for the state at all levels and the ruling classes it represents to paint the Maoist movement into an illegal corner and successfully delegitimise it as an external threat to popular sovereignty.

The Maoists doubtless have a significant numerical and ideological presence within the PCPA and the wider Lalgarh movement. But the committee, which is much more diverse in its broad Left ideological composition, is far from being a front of the Maoist group. And that, as far as the Maoist commitment to a militant working-class movement is concerned, would have spelt no harm. If anything, the Maoists and their sympathisers in Lalgarh ought to have envisaged such a situation as an opportunity for them to continue to work quietly within the PCPA and provide the insurrectionary movement with requisite logistical support and ideological orientation to expand politically to engage with and integrate a multitude of other disenfranchised and exploited sections of West Bengal's society and economy such as the embattled peasants of Nandigram, Rajbongshi separatists of north Bengal plains, the Gorkhas of Darjeeling and the large masses of workers rendered unemployed by the sharp decline in the fortunes of the state's tea and jute industries. This process of integration through continuous engagement would have had to address the specific concerns of each of those sections even as it transformed their mutually competitive idioms of political articulation into a coherent but multitudinous critique of the logic of the larger political economy responsible for all their various miseries. That would lead, not to an aggregative programme of social change, but render Maoism into an ideological current that is always internal to an ever-growing constellation of popular movements.

In such circumstances, the modality of political violence would always be that of popular insurrection. And even guerrilla tactics, as and when they are deployed, would necessarily be envisaged as an integral part of this insurrectionary paradigm. That would not only make it hard for the state to delegitimise such violence as illegal or the movements that generate them as anti-sovereign, it would also ensure that Maoism is rescued from the excesses of its current sectarian militarism that have, often enough, ended up replicating the same configurations of alienated state power, which the movement has sought to unravel.

Clearly, the Maoists can avoid tactical blunders like the one they have committed in Lalgarh only when they re-frame their political-organisational vision. Their obsession with territorial expansion, which has spelt no real political-ideological breakthrough for the larger working-class movement, essentially stems from the Maoists' insistence on envisaging the party as an a priori state-form, which seeks to subordinate the singularity of various experiences of disaffection and registers of struggle to its doctrinaire conception of politics, which is no more than the overgeneralisation of one particular experience of social oppression and resistance. What they need to do, instead, is to imagine the organisation as a movement-form, wherein Maoism is a dynamic organisational impulse and the party is always in a state of bottom-up formation through a perpetual process of politicisation at the grassroots.

West Bengal, ironically enough, provides the most conducive political climate for the Maoists to effect such a reorientation. Their struggles against a repressive state, controlled for over three decades by a coalition of Left forces helmed by the largest Communist Party, ought to compel them to reflect on how communist-left forces, which were once the undisputed principal representatives of a genuine working-class movement, have come to distort it beyond recognition.

The degeneration of the CPI(M)-led LF, contrary to the popular belief shaped by the neo-liberal consensus, is not because of its failure to turn fully social democratic but precisely because it has abandoned the tortuous dirt-path of working-class struggle for the comfortable highway of social democracy. Social democracy, which envisages social progress and the well-being of the working people and the poor essentially as a question of distributive justice, is a form of governance that seeks to equitably distribute a given basket of socio-economic entitlements. In such a 'Leftist' scheme, there is no place for interventionist and transformative politics because the state, which for social democracy is an instrument of efficient regulation and equitable redistribution, is treated as a passive and neutral entity that must be captured and then merely controlled.

The state, however, is in reality constitutive of an exploitative, oppressive and hierarchical social order. To that extent, a radical socialist programme must actively articulate the tendency to erode, not capture, it. For, it is only through such erosion that the structural reinforcement of a stratified society can be undermined. The preposterous contradiction the CPI(M)-led LF has created between industrial development that is inescapable, and universal democracy that is indispensable, is a symptom of its social-democratic degeneration. Its failure to imagine more democratic and participatory configurations of socio-political power, which could drive truly cooperative consolidation of land and other resources, and posit an alternative model of development, is because of its social-democratic fixation on the state.

That the Maoists too should call themselves the CPI(M)—Communist Party of India (Maoist)—is uncanny. But more eerie perhaps is the fact that their conception of the party as a state-form predisposes them to a social democratic approach to politics that virtually makes them a mirror-image of the original CPI(M). It is time the Maoists woke up and smelt their gunpowder.

13

Three Fragmentary Theses on the Politico-theoretical Problematic posed by the Current Phase of the Indian Maoist Movement for Working Class Politics

I

The question of overcoming the problem of systemic cooption that faces the Maoist insurgency raging in certain tribal and preponderantly agrarian (in the sense of socio-occupational geography) areas of the country is essentially a question of how to beat the legal-illegal dichotomy that is constitutive of capitalism—a system made possible only in and through contradictions—and its horizon of legality. (This threat of cooption confronts the current Maoist movement—as it indeed would and does any movement against the ways and codes of dominant institutions that regulate and reinforce the various sectors of capitalist life—either in the form of the movement being determined and articulated by the dualised logic of capitalist regulation that compels it to envisage itself as responding to a war while fighting it; or in the form of being accommodated by and within the given form/forms of the capitalist state.) This question, of course in being posed but also in being answered, also gives rise to a corollary in that it posits the problematic of how a workers' opposition to a state formed through revolutionary eruption can, because of such opposition and not despite it, retain its working-class orientation. To get back to the Maoist movement, the problem of its subsumption by capitalism—manifest either as its cooption within the given capitalist state-forms or in its determination and articulation by the dualised logic of the capitalist state even as it is apparently still in its movemental moment—can be effectively dealt with and beaten only when the 'illegal' ontology, which is seeking to become yet another law in and through its dualism-articulated struggle against the prevailing law to displace it from its legitimate place to occupy it, is challenged from within its own zone where it has already become, both structurally and functionally, the law. Before we proceed any further we would do well to realise that an ontology of working-class resistance, which is designated as illegal within the dualised horizon of capitalist legality, is an ontology that in its formation is an expression of the tendency to transgress and unravel the horizon of capitalist legality and thus move beyond the legal-illegal duality and contradiction it constitutively engenders. But this ontology gets designated (or symbolised) as 'illegal' because of its struggle against the prevailing law, which maintains and reinforces the capitalist horizon of conflict and contradiction that the struggle of this ontology in its formation seeks to transcend. Simply put, the foundational translegal or law-unraveling manoeuvre of an ontology of resistance comes to be designated as illegal because of the inescapable duality inherent in all struggles, of which its specific struggling orientation too is an intrinsic part. The recognition of the necessity of this duality, to paraphrase Engels, is constitutive of the freedom called dialectic.

But the only way this endogenous challenge against the law-constituting structure and function of the 'illegal' ontology at its own location can become truly translegal—which would mean it does not acquiesce to or align with the established law against which the 'illegal' is ranged—is when the given horizon of capitalist 'legality' that is maintained and reinforced by the established law is sought to be decimated through a proliferating series of determinate and simultaneous challenges to it at its various multiple locations. These challenges, needless to say, are specific manoeuvres to overcome the capitalist horizon of the legal and the legal-illegal dichotomy it constitutively engenders at each of those respective specific locations. These challenges or manoeuvres, in their continuous proliferation, come to constitute the totality of the horizon of trans-capitalist process, which is the inverse opposite (negativity) of the capitalist horizon of legality and ontological fixities. This real horizon of continuous motion, in emerging as an inversely opposite (negative) alternative to the symbolist horizon of ontological fixities through critical transcendence and displacement of the latter, and its constitutive logic of duality, overcomes, in terms of concrete situation, the state and the law. That, clearly, renders the twin or binary conceptions of legal-illegal redundant. This is the theoretical essence of Marx's idea of "revolution in permanence", which Mao Zedong complemented through refoundation in the Chinese conditions through his formulation of the "two-line struggle". Such an understanding, and its deployment, brings to fore and makes one sensitive to the ineluctable operation of dual power in a working-class revolutionary struggle. It, therefore, indicates why it is impossible to conceive of completing a socialist revolution in one country, or one socio-occupational geographic zone, to the exclusion of all else.

II

To grasp this impossibility and go beyond it—especially with regard to the current Maoist movement being stuck in its 'original' tribal-peasant socio-occupational zones—we need to understand that the history of capitalism is a history of contradictions. Its various moments are, as a consequence, pitted against each other, even as each of those moments are constituted by contradictions and duality that are determinate (or specific) in terms of their respective formal configurations of the general political economy of alienating and competitive capitalism. So, the universal political-economic logic of contradiction and duality, which constitutes the specific forms of such contradictions and duality in particular moments of history—which in turn have been particularised and have thus congealed into conflictive locations with regard to one another—has to be grasped in its determinateness. Therefore, the theoretical (subjective or vanguardist) outside, which was envisaged by Lenin in his attempt to theorise the party in *What is to be Done* and which has been integral to the Leninist practice ever since, must be seen as the expression of the one in a determinate moment of contradictory and dualised history of capitalism. The ontological form through which the logic of the one expresses itself at a determinate moment should, precisely because of its determinateness, be seen as specific to that moment and therefore provisional. It must not be mistaken, as it often is both by the upholders and detractors of Leninist vanguardism, for a transhistorical ontology, which actually implies the imposition of a form that expresses the logic of the one at particular historical moment of contradiction and duality on another logically similar but historically (and thus idiomatically) different moment of capitalism.

Each of these historically different moments of capital must, however, be seen as arising internally from one another through a process of internal motion that is wrought by determinate subjective interventions in their momentary and thus ontic specificity. This motion is really a process of quantitative changes (at the historical-formal level) leading to a qualitative mutation of and rupture from that given historical form or idiom. This will obviate the Althusserian absolutisation of relative autonomy of various moments or levels of the lived history of capitalism. Althusser's idea of relative autonomy is productive when we are envisaging intervention at specific moments in their determinateness but not when we see the entire capitalist system in the totality of the process it must become in order to supersede itself. In other words, the determinate intervention at a specific historical moment must be seen to be giving rise to a new moment of duality that must be intervened in if the spirit of the preceding intervention—overcoming duality and contradiction to obtain to the one—is to be sustained by discerning the logic of that prior intervention in the new moment into which the preceding one has unfolded and in the process has obscured the possibility of relocating that logic by dislocating it. So, intervention has to be envisaged both in terms of the given segmentised and fragmentary stasis of the capitalist system and the internal continuity of its own motion. This means that the former type of intervention needs to be correlated with and envisaged as the latter. For, that is how it actually is, and must be seen, refracted through the prism of terms of its own logic of transcending segmentised duality to obtain to the one—the process expressed and constituted through and in the critical manoeuvre of dissolving its preceding congealed momentary appearances.

III

B.T. Ranadive's 'Russian' and 'Trotskyite' line during the Telangana movement of accomplishing revolution through general strike and mass insurrection in the cities is, in the context of the failure of the current Maoist insurgency to move beyond its tribal-peasant bases, particularly valid today. The practitioners of this line must, however, know that its validity is contingent on the line not falling into the undialectical and partial (Laclauian) trap of envisaging itself as privileged over the Maoists' model of agrarian (New Democratic) revolution, which is fully valid within its own determinate socio-occupational geography. This line must, in its articulation, see itself in constellational continuity with the localised, momentary anti-capitalist form of the Maoist agrarian revolutionary movement only insofar as that form emerges as an expression of the trans-capitalist and thus processual constitutive logic at that historical moment or location of the rural-tribal-agrarian. The form in question is an expression of the trans-capitalist processual logic in its formative and enunciative moment and this moment must, therefore, be distinguished from the congealed, institutionalised moment of the form when/where the formalised content or the logic of the form per se dominates. (This constellational logic could be understood through Henri Lefebvre's recognition of "revolution lagging behind itself"; or in an Adornoesque-Benjaminian vein articulated as the momentary forms of the revolutionary process being registered and grasped as the various afterimages of its processual essence. This constellational logic could also be stated in Althusserian terms by envisaging the various localised or momentary forms of the working-class struggle as traces or effects of their respective foundational encounters in order to overcome the necessity those forms exude in their particularity of being free and floating signifiers.) This constellational logic of revolution is conceptualised in Antonies Negri's Spinozist-Marxist idea of the multitude, which rightly sees the historical forms or socio-occupational subjects enacting the singular logic called the working class multiple. This naturally renders the party of the working class movemental, and the vanguard dynamically hierarchical. Many of our current comrades, who kind of propose the Ranadive line of urban strikes leading up to a mass insurrection as a ground from which to critique the Maoists, make precisely the same non-constellational, 'workerist' (sectionalist) mistake as committed by Ranadive in the context of the Telangana peasant movement of the undivided CPI in the late forties and early fifties.

Their critique of Mao's model of agrarian revolution and his formulation of "New Democracy" is plagued by the same problem for they are unable to see how those anti-capitalist forms—which Mao posed at a specific, Chinese moment of the unfolding of the global revolutionary process—have been constituted through the determinate enactment of the trans-capitalist and trans-ontological processual logic in the specificity of their socio-occupational, political geographic and historico-temporal moment. This error could, however, be averted if Mao's Chinese Revolution is seen, not as a one-time occurrence that ended in 1949, but is instead situated in constellational continuity with Mao's praxes embodied in what has subsequently come to be known as "The Great Leap Forward" and the "Great Proletarian Cultural Revolution" and which constituted the unfolding of the revolutionary logic of Mao's China that had congealed in the state form through the 'seizure' of power by the Communist Party of China in 1949 precisely because of that congealment. These two moments of Mao's praxis can be clearly seen to be embodying (or performing) his idea of what he called "continuous revolution". [Mao explicated this theory of his in, among other places, a speech to Supreme State Conference on January 28, 1958, where he clearly stated, "I advocate the theory of the permanent revolution. You must not think that this is Trotsky's theory of the permanent revolution. In making revolution, one must strike while the iron is hot, one revolution following another; the revolution must advance without interruption...." He expanded on this formulation in his Sixty Articles on Work Methods when he wrote, "ideological and political struggle among men as well as revolution will continue to exist forever and universally...".] Clearly then, this theory of Mao's was a re-enactment of Marx's formulation of "revolution in permanence". [See Marx's *The Class Struggles in France 1848 to 1850* for this formulation.]

Mao's continuous revolution was nothing but the codification of the practice of mobilisation—through "The Great Leap Forward" and the Cultural Revolution—of the emerging new social subject of working-class politics to critically undermine and supersede the inevitable institutionalisation and congealment of his earlier "New Democratic" moment of the trans-capitalist revolutionary process. That, in phenomenological terms, meant the waging of struggle to eliminate the nomenklatura and "capitalist roaders" in the party. The nomenklatura and capitalist roaders can, generally speaking, be designated as the bureaucratised elite of a Communist Party when it ceases to be a movement-form to become a state-form. In the specific instance of Mao's China, this elite, which signified the restoration of capitalism through its embodiment of the differential (and thus bourgeois) configuration of class power, had been formed as a result of the congealment, institutionalisation and statisation of the global revolutionary process enunciated by and constitutive of the form of the Communist Party of China at its New Democratic moment. [Though these moments of revolution have, in the specific experience and praxis of Mao's China, turned out to be posed in the frame of successive temporality, that is not necessarily how revolutionary moments would always become discernible. Our position vis-à-vis the Maoist movement here, for instance, shows that different moments ripe for revolutionary, working-class intervention inhabit the same temporal moment (in scalar terms) of a temporality that empirically has just the vector (or teleology) of capitalism, but are separated in their being located within different socio-occupational geographies. The overgeneralisation that the Indian Maoists have been effecting through their dogmatic and Stalinised adherence to the formalisation of the revolutionary experience and practice in the New Democratic, agrarian revolutionary moment of Mao's China has led to the conflation of the processual revolutionary essence and the form that essence constituted in the process of expressing itself determinately at a specific moment of its unfolding. This has meant the undermining of the processual, historico-logical or, what Moishe Postone calls the quasi-objective, character of the revolutionary operation. That has, not surprisingly, brought the Indian Maoists and some of their 'workerist' critics on the same page in terms of the theoretical approach they have adopted to expand the current Maoist movement or in criticising this endeavour respectively. The tenor of the latter's rejection of Mao's and the Maoist forms of intervention indicates they are not willing to distinguish the dualising logic of those forms per se in their moment of congealment from the processual revolutionary logic they constitutively express. They throw the baby with the bathwater even as the Maoists, whom they seek to criticise, envisage the bathwater itself to be the baby.]

To come back to the praxis of continuous revolution in revolutionary China, the Mao who is a living, practising embodiment of this idea of continuous revolution is many as each time he is organic to the multiple, constellationally bound—essentially united and therefore formally conflicted—social subjects of the working-class logic. Thus Mao's emphasis on constantly occupying the antithetical position—so much so that in his understanding of the dialectic there is no moment of synthesis—(Žižek on Mao in *In Defence of Lost Causes*) renders his individuality into that of a trans-subjective revolutionary, which is composed of both his institutionalisation and his own iconoclasm vis-à-vis the congealment of his preceding revolutionary selves. His practice led to the Communist Party of China being envisaged as a horizon of movement-form that is constitutive of the unfolding of the constant dialectical dance of congealment and decongealment; institutionalisation and deinstitutionalisation; revolution-restoration-and-revolution; and negation, negation of negation, negation of negation of negation ad infinitum. The Indian Maoists' claim that they are capable of repeating Mao on this score is erroneous as their conceptualisation of the Maoist path flows from their reification of Mao's specific experience of revolutionary moments in the form of linear temporal succession of stages.

As a result, they fail to see the many subjectivities embodied in Mao the individual in multiple moments that are in logical continuity through and because of the conflict of their congealed momentary forms with one another. Thus the assertion of various intellectuals, sympathetic to the CPI (Maoist), to make the logic of the Maoist movement unfold is nothing but a proposal to spread 'Maoism' through the overgeneralisation of the locally valid and localised experience and resultant practice of the CPI (Maoist) in its tribal-agrarian socio-occupational zones. Such a proposal implies, tendentially, the authoritarian and coercive imposition of the party and its 'revolution' as state-forms on a heterogeneity of working-class experiences. This is clearly a Blanquist programme of envisaging revolution in terms of capturing the twin and constitutively twinned spheres of circulation and regulation without transforming the sphere of capitalist production through the decimation of value creation, which is a constant realisation of the tendency to make the state and its function of distributing value wither away. For, the persistence or emergence of the state, and the circulation-distribution spheres that it is constitutively integral to, retroactively implies the creation and extraction of value at the point of production. Such a Blanquist strategy, needless to say, undermines the communist invariant of the one (revolutionary process) a la Alain Badiou (*Saint Paul: The Foundation of Universalism*) and restores capitalism and its foundational logic of dualised contradiction, existence of classes and (class) differences, and class domination.